Management Skills Series
Managing for Success

Managing for Success

A Human Approach

ALFRED YORK

CASSELL

IN ASSOCIATION WITH THE INSTITUTE FOR SUPERVISION AND MANAGEMENT

Cassell
Wellington House   215 Park Avenue South
125 Strand   New York
London WC2R 0BB   NY 10003

British Library Cataloguing-in-Publication Data
A catalogue record for this book is available from the British
Library.

Library of Congress Cataloging-in-Publication Data
York, Alfred, 1922–
      Managing for success   /   Alfred York.
         p.   cm. – (Management skills series)
      "In association with the Institute for Supervision and
Management."
      Includes index.
      ISBN 0–304–33316–6 (pbk.)   : $26.00
      1.   Management.   2.   Interpersonal communication.
      3.   Organizational   effectiveness.   I.   Title.
      II.   Series: Management skills series (London)
HD31.Y58   1995   94–43420
658.4–dc20   CIP

Typeset by York House Typographic Ltd.
Printed and bound in Great Britain by Redwood Books,
Trowbridge, Wiltshire

Contents

Foreword

The last decade has seen significant changes in management in British manufacturing industry and these are now being experienced in other sectors of the economy. Despite these changes, senior management has still, in many cases, failed to realise the necessity to equip first level managers for the new working environment.

This does not necessarily mean that managers need formal updating on their human resource skills, but it certainly does require that they have access to some *vade mecum* to which they can refer. In developing this series of books in association with Cassell, the Institute is providing those at the critical interface of management with the practical guidance they need.

This book, the second in the series, does not set out to be a formal textbook for management. Instead, it seeks to focus the manager's vision on the main themes which he or she should address in the critical area of managing people. I believe, through its informal approach, it gets over the importance of that area of responsibility in a way which is far more relevant than the majority of other bodies in this field.

If nothing else, the author has proved, beyond doubt, the need for managers to be equipped to meet the challenge. This can only be achieved through knowing themselves and their responsibilities – a position which he sums up in the axiom: 'If you fail to prepare, prepare to fail.'

While change may mean that managers do not know precisely what to prepare *for*, they, nevertheless, need to understand the basic tenets of dealing with the most important resource they will ever have to handle – the human resource!

Alfred York has combined a wise understanding of human resource skills such a manager requires, with examples which can be readily appreciated by those at the sharp end of management. I think that all those who read this book – whether members of the ISM or those in the wider field of management – will find it both useful and, equally important, most readable.

G.L.D. Alderson
Director
ISM

Author's Introduction

Profound changes in the pattern of working life have been a world-wide phenomenon of the twentieth century. A hundred or more years ago most people lived a rural, agricultural existence. Today all over the world their descendants live in big cities and their suburbs. They work in towering office blocks and may travel long distances between home and work. The evolution of an industrial society has produced very significant consequences for human relationships at work. No longer working in the fields alongside relatives or fellow villagers, people nowadays work with other people whom they would normally never have met but for the chance of employment by the same organization. These relationships with others are in a state of constant flux as people move from one job to another. The enormous changes in working life have produced problems that were not nearly as evident in former times, when working life was much more simple.

To achieve organizational aims and objectives work-colleagues need to collaborate harmoniously with each other as well as with other groups in the organization, with clients and any others who have contacts with the employing organization. The various functional groups and divisions that form the whole organization all need to be pulling in the same direction.

We all know that the ideal of complete harmony and collaboration is seldom, if ever, achieved. Work-colleagues in the same group often do not see eye-to-eye. One group or division may be in conflict with another. Human relations are a constant cause of problems in a complex, industrial society. It has always been so, and we may predict with confidence that so long as people continue to work together in groups and organizations, problems of human relationships will remain. How far the expenditure of this unfruitful energy gets out of control or is channelled into more profitable and productive directions depends very much on those who lead work-groups at all levels.

Leaders of work-groups, large and small, have the vital role of welding individuals into motivated, collaborative, productive teams. Without leadership to give direction, monitor progress, exhort and encourage, keep teams on course, deal with problems of human relationships, inefficiency and discipline, groups could well remain as a disorganized, squabbling rabble.

With the benefit of the experience of more than a hundred years of industrial life, these conclusions doubtless appear too trite and obvious to state. Be that as it may. The history of industrial enterprise up to and including the present times indicates in general that insufficient attention has been given to the importance of an organization's human resources and especially to effective leadership. Human problems at work still keep industrial tribunals busy. So whilst most of us know what the problems are and perhaps how they may, at least, be mitigated, managers still need to be constantly reminded of the crucial importance of the human aspects of their job and of what they need to know and do to be effective leaders of work-groups.

The ideas described in this book are the product of a very varied working life spanning fifty years in the UK and overseas. It has included managing at all levels, training managers and trainers, consultancy assignments and postgraduate study of management and its human aspects – my specialist field. It has been one long learning process, which is still continuing.

This experience has led to firm beliefs about the crucial importance of good leadership in the management of people and about the means by which it might be achieved. Of course my views are in no way unique, but it has been encouraging to learn that the conclusions of research confirm what my own experience has taught me.

There is now extensive literature about management and its related subjects. It is pertinent to ask, therefore, what one more book on the subject could say that has not already been said many times over. In general terms my own views and conclusions do not diverge from the common consensus about the importance of the effective management of people to organizational success. The differences between one text and another are seldom about basic philosophy. They mostly concern emphases. The particular purposes of this book are these:

1. To emphasize yet again how important it is to manage people effectively for the achievement of organizational goals and the satisfaction of individual employees.

2. To offer what I hope might be useful advice on the approach and practice that my own experience has shown to be effective. In the course of extensive reading of the subject I have regularly come across new ideas and new slants that challenge my assumptions, stimulate thinking and influence my behaviour and practice of management. I hope that what I have to say may have a similar value.

3. To propose that:

   (a) effective management of people ultimately depends on sound judgements about the suitability of applicants for appointment, the performance and behaviour of employees and any action needed for change and improvement;

   (b) sound judgements are based on systematic practice – the definition of the requirements for effective performance and the evidence of actual performance and behaviour.

4. To encourage readers, perhaps, to examine their own competence and needs in the management of people and to take whatever action they consider to be necessary and appropriate.

The contents of the book and the treatment of the subject are logically derived from these purposes. Chapters 1–4 cover the basic knowledge and skills that managers need to use in some form or other every day for effective practice in the management of people. Chapters 5–11 cover the particular personnel tasks for which the knowledge and skills are needed. All of these tasks are important to organizational effectiveness, but selecting the right employees and developing their abilities are especially important, I would suggest. Accordingly, I have given these subjects particular emphasis and attention.

Whenever I am conducting training courses in the subjects covered in this book, I involve trainees participatively as much as possible. They have experience of managing or being managed, which good trainers use for learning purposes. I regret that authors cannot have a similar involvement with their readers, who normally have a passive role. Nevertheless, I propose to involve readers of this book as far as is practicable and possible and according to their wishes.

At the beginning of each chapter I have set out what seem to me to be the basic questions that need to be addressed. They indicate the issues to be covered: they also provide readers with an opportunity to consider what their own answers would be before reading the chapter and comparing their thoughts with mine. Continuing the participative approach, I have appended exercises at the end of each chapter as tests of knowledge and learning. Some of these may be suitable for use with colleagues or members of managers' work-groups. I have produced and used these exercises for many years and have tested their efficacy. Whether readers wish to participate or not is entirely a matter for their own choice. If they do not wish to do so, then they can simply read the text and leave it at that.

This is not a text for students following courses of academic study. It does not, therefore, include detailed accounts of the many theories that have been produced about the management of people at work. The book is intended mainly for junior managers and supervisors as a guide to effective practice. The word 'manager' is used throughout to include anyone responsible for leading a work-group.

I have purposely included a number of anecdotes based on the experience of myself, colleagues and acquaintances to illustrate various points, and at the same time to add colour and interest.

Finally, few books, if any, are produced by authors alone and unaided. This book is no exception, I would like to record my gratitude to the following people: Naomi Roth of the publishers Cassell PLC; Gordon Alderson, Director of the Institute for Supervision and Management, for support and advice; and Susan Vince for efficient typing of the manuscript.

Alfred York
Poole, Dorset
December 1994

CHAPTER 1

Understanding Behaviour

BASIC QUESTIONS

 1 What are the influences and factors that shape each individual?
 2 What are values and attitudes?
 3 What is motivation? Why has it received special attention in the study of human behaviour?
 4 Why is it important for managers to be aware of the effects of their own behaviour?
 5 By what means might awareness of self be developed?
 6 What are the common characteristics of group behaviour?
 7 What effects can group-membership have on individuals?
 8 What is meant by leadership style?
 9 Is any one style likely to be more effective than another? Why?
 10 What are the characteristics of the ideal manager-leader?

(1) INDIVIDUALS

People are identical inasmuch as they share the same general physical and mental characteristics. At the same time, each individual is a unique product of genetic and environmental influences. We are all born with individual sets of characteristics and are then continuously influenced for the rest of our lives through contacts with other people and a variety of experiences, e.g. parents, other relatives, friends, teachers, religious leaders, work colleagues, education, training, books, films, work-jobs and so on. Life is a process of continual learning, modification and change. Depending on factors such as intelligence and sensitivity, some people are more disposed to learn than others. No human being, however, can avoid the influences that come from the external environment. The effects of these influences on behaviour are not always perceived at the conscious level. Individuals may change their behaviour without being aware that another person or experience has initiated the change. What kinds of effects might these external influences have on individual behaviour? They might shape values, attitudes, perceptions, motivation, judgements and decisions. Clearly, managers cannot be expected to psychoanalyse each member of their work-groups. To be effective, however, they do need to understand the complexities of behaviour, the effects of external influences and of individual differences on the ways the members of their work-groups behave and interact.

Values and Attitudes

Values are important determinants of behaviour. For example, somebody who values peace and quiet would probably prefer to remain living in a quiet rural environment than to live and work in a big, noisy city, even if this means forgoing opportunities for employment, income, prestige, etc. The person who values status above all else will probably seek a career that offers opportunities to meet this desire and will then be strongly motivated to satisfy this need. People are not always aware of their values. These can be assessed by what people do and the decisions they make. They are often revealed when people have to make a choice between two conflicting options such as the following example. Someone has been offered promotion with all that this means in terms of career prospects. It also involves moving to a distant, less pleasant location and the disruption of family life. Should he or she accept or remain in the present pleasant location without disrupting family life, children's education, etc.? Values could be seen as the price that people are prepared to pay to achieve what they want.

Attitudes are also important determinants of behaviour. They could be described as a more or less stable set of opinions affecting people's reactions to particular situations, subjects and people. If we already know somebody's attitude towards a particular situation, we might be able to make a fairly accurate prediction of how he or she would react to another, similar situation. Prejudices are particular forms of attitudes, where the mind is resistant to challenging evidence. Attitudes can change over time. People who had a hostile attitude to foreigners might modify this view when their daughter makes a happy marriage with someone from a foreign country. Attitudes are an important element affecting the effective performance of work. People need knowledge and skills, but if these are not accompanied by the appropriate positive attitudes the effectiveness of performance may be seriously diminished.

Motivation

Motivation is the impetus that drives people to behave in various ways and to seek to fulfil a variety of needs. Because employers need to know 'what makes people tick', motivation of people at work has received particular and continuous attention in research studies. Certain authors, such as Mayo, Maslow, Herzberg, McGregor and McLelland, have achieved universal fame for their studies of the subject. Without research of this kind, managers would probably not have given the importance of motivation much thought and would doubtless have gone on assuming that money was the main motivator. The theories that motivation-studies have produced vary in their emphasis and conclusions, but there is a general consensus:

1. Motivation is a force that drives people to satisfy needs.
2. Needs that people seek to satisfy are common to all human beings, such as physical needs – to satisfy hunger and thirst, to find shelter, etc.; social needs – the need for the company of others; the need to be esteemed and valued by other people; the need for self-fulfilment, to achieve something perceived as worthwhile, to be creative.
3. The motivational force has three basic elements: a direction towards specific goals; intensity, depending on particular individual desires; duration – the force may be short or long-lasting. It may be terminated when a need is satisfied and transferred to new goals.
4. Motivation is the result of an individual's cost-benefit analysis, i.e. people have to perceive what for them is a worthwhile benefit before investing the necessary effort to achieve an outcome. These decisions are affected by personal value-systems.

Those who manage groups at work need to be aware of the complexity of motivation. They may not be able to satisfy the needs of each indi-vidual, but they can create a climate in which the members of the group perceive a worthwhile outcome for the efforts and commitment they are required to give.

(2) SELF-AWARENESS

The need for self-awareness is a recurring theme in the literature on human behaviour. Its importance has been emphasized since the earliest times. For example, the precept 'Know thyself' was written in gold above the portico of the temple of Apollo in ancient Greece. More recently, Robert Burns' well-known lines in the poem *To a Louse* have commented on the importance of self-awareness: 'O wad some power the giftie gie us, to see oursels as ithers see us, it wad frae mony a blunder free us, and foolish notion'. Since self-awareness is held to be so important to successful behaviour, it seems worthwhile and logical to examine why it is important, what it means and how it might be achieved.

Self-awareness is important both personally and interpersonally, i.e. in terms of decisions that individuals need to make for themselves, affecting their own lives and careers, and in terms of their relationships with other people.

In personal terms, awareness of one's capabilities and limitations is particularly valuable in a number of work situations, such as employment selection, career development, performance-appraisal, training and development. It is conventional to assume that in these situations prospective employers, managers, personnel managers and trainers take the leading part in making the major decisions, whilst the individual is relegated to a passive role. However, attitudes are changing and the value of encouraging individuals to take more responsibility for themselves is becoming increasingly apparent, for example in assessing their own suitability for employment, choosing their career paths, assessing their own work performance and identifying their own needs for further experience and training. Therefore, to reach sound decisions affecting their personal lives people need to have clear and balanced views about where their talents lie, what their weaknesses might be and what their needs are for further development and improvement.

The greater part of human life is interpersonal. It is spent largely in domestic, working and social relationships. Although effective collaboration and communication are regularly acknowledged as essential to successful living and to the achievement of the goals of human enterprise, the evidence of frustrated effort and conflict is abundant and abiding. Much time is devoted, therefore, in management training to these problems, to the diagnosis of causes and the prescription of remedies. Undoubtedly, lack of self-awareness by individuals and the consequences for interpersonal relationships are major reasons for human problems in collaborating and communicating effectively. The universal difficulties that people have in relating to others can only mean that most of us rarely, if ever, pause to consider our own part in human relationships, the effects that our behaviour might have on others, the extent to which we might be contributing to any difficulties that have arisen and the positive steps that we might take that could lead to improvement.

Self-awareness in interpersonal terms concerns perceptions – the individual's view of self and views held by others. Each person has an image of self which is seldom the result of any conscious, systematic analysis and is most unlikely to be explicitly expressed by the individual. Any clues to the self-image are more likely to be made by others, e.g. 'She fancies herself' or 'He lacks confidence'. Thus, in addition to what might be loosely described as the individual's semi-conscious image of self, all the other people who know the individual in a wide range of situations – at home, at work and socially will have a view of the individual built up from casual observations of behaviour, assumptions and their own interpretations of motives. With a wide range of situations and relationships there will obviously be some agreements and disagreements of view. The individual's view of self may be in conflict with a consensus amongst all other acquaintances. There may be differences amongst the acquaintances depending on the chemistry of their personal relationships with the individual and their own values, attitudes and motives.

These perceptual differences and possible conflicts are summarized in the model known as the Johari Window (named after its psychologist authors – Joe Luft and Harry Ingham). The window has four 'panes' describing the views of behaviour of self and others:

1. known to self and to others (public);
2. known to others but not to self (blind);
3. known to self but not to others (hidden);
4. not known to self nor to others.

If self-awareness is to be used as a significant, positive force for developing and improving individuals, helping them to make sound decisions for life and working careers, and to develop important skills in interpersonal relationships, it is not enough simply to describe the basic facts about the image of self, the views held by others and the possibility of perceptual agreement and disagreement. We need to consider what it requires in practice. Self-awareness should imply that the individual:

- has reached a balanced and as honest a view as possible of his/her abilities and limitations without overestimating or underestimating self;
- is aware that his/her behaviour always has effects on others and may, therefore, regularly need modification to achieve effective communication and relationships;
- takes positive steps to ascertain the views of others about his/her behaviour and takes particular note of any consensus of views.

The final and most difficult question to answer is how self-awareness of this kind may be achieved. As we have seen, there will always be casually formed images produced both by the individual and by others. Because ultimately the image of self depends on subjective human perception and judgements, there cannot be one absolute, true image of self. It is a question of relativity – some images are more accurate than others. So how can any kind of truth about a person be reached? The truest guide will always come from the actual behaviour. A person's image of self might, for example, include patience as one of the plus points. But this may well represent what the person would like to be rather than how he/she actually behaves. A careful analysis of actual behaviour might reveal considerably more evidence of impatient behaviour than the individual is prepared to believe. Even then, there are still problems. Because the individual is apparently blind to this defect, it would need to be pointed out by another person. This could well develop into the abiding problem of definition and criteria that always bedevils judgement of human behaviour, i.e. a debate and possible disagreement about what patient or impatient behaviour is, and what would be acceptable evidence of this behaviour in practice.

Despite this basic, inevitable problem, the surest route to establishing any kind of truth about the individual's make-up is a systematic analysis of actual past behaviour with the aim of producing as much significant evidence as possible about values, attitudes, motivation, capabilities, limitations, preferences, and needs for future development, i.e.:

1. Identify the major influences and events that have developed the individual's knowledge, skills, values and attitudes and have helped to shape the personality, e.g. family, education, work, social life and spare time pursuits, reading, travel, and so on.
2. On this basis, determine what conclusions the events and decisions of life reveal about the person, i.e. knowledge and skills acquired, values and attitudes developed, personality traits, motivational forces, likes

and dislikes, work and pursuits for which the person is best and least suited.

3. Produce a summary of personality traits, capabilities, limitations and need for further development.

The analysis can be carried out by the individual, but it does require system, discipline and, above all, an honest and balanced appraisal of one's own personality and behaviour – the essence of the dilemma to which Burns referred. The analysis can be enhanced with the help of another person who has developed counselling skills and can, therefore, ask open and relevant questions and can listen sensitively. In a helpful and friendly manner the counsellor can ask the probing and awkward questions that the individual may prefer to avoid. He or she can tune in to feelings and emotions, reveal values, attitudes and motivational forces that underlie behaviour, and thus help the individual to reach a balanced view of capabilities, limitations and needs.

It is also necessary and salutary to ascertain the views of a range of acquaintances who know the individual in a variety of situations – domestically, socially, at work and through leisure pursuits. There are obvious difficulties with external assessments of this kind – in persuading people to undertake the task in the first place, getting them to carry out a systematic analysis, but most of all persuading them to say what they truly think – which can be especially difficult or embarrassing when the conclusions are likely to be unpalatable.

Those who can be persuaded to undertake the difficult task of assessing the individual could be asked to assume the role of a confidential referee and to produce a summarized picture of the individual's capabilities and limitations in terms of knowledge, skills and personal traits. The subject of the analysis should then study the comments of the reporting acquaintances and make a careful note and comparison of views, in particular the similarities and differences. The significant questions that need to be asked are: In what areas do these reports mainly agree? How do these comments compare with views of self? If there are any differences between the views of self and the consensus of other people's views, why is this, and what does it indicate? What actions, if any, do the conclusions of self-analysis indicate?

Whilst self-awareness is generally important for the personal and interpersonal purposes already described, it has a special importance for the many people whose work in any way involves leadership. By the very nature of their work they are much concerned with the behaviour of others, with their needs for behavioural changes and the methods by which these changes might be achieved. To have any basis for claiming insight into the behaviour of others, for helping them to change and sometimes even demanding change, they must surely begin with knowledge of themselves and especially the impact that they have on others.

The Video Arts film – *The Unorganised Manager* – provides an impressive example of this problem. The central figure is a manager who is totally unaware of his shortcomings and of the adverse effects he has on all the people with whom he comes into contact – work-colleagues, customers and family. When these are revealed by everyone with whom he has close and regular contacts, he cannot believe his ears.

The only people who can give managers reliable feedback about their style at the work-place are those most affected by it – the members of their work-groups. For obvious reasons this is a very tricky situation. Old-fashioned autocrats would turn in their graves at the very thought of inviting subordinates to comment on their behaviour and performance. Some feedback might be possible during performance-appraisal discussions. If managers ask people directly – What do you think of me as a manager? – they are unlikely to get very helpful answers. Many would, no doubt, find the question very disconcerting and would avoid telling their managers what they truly and honestly think. A few might overstep the bounds of tactful behaviour. So the manager's questions have to be less threatening, i.e.: Is there any way in which I could help you more than I do already? Is there anything that I do that causes you problems? Even these questions could receive circumspect replies. A number of organizations have set up feedback systems, whereby members of staff provide written comments, anonymously of course, about their managers' behaviour and performance. It might seem like a revolutionary idea, likely to cause all kinds of problems in relationships between managers and their staffs. However, a consensus of views should not be ignored. It should certainly open some managers' eyes and give them food for thought. It might also help to prevent incompetent leaders being promoted, because senior management are more aware of a group leader's impact on his or her work-group than they would otherwise be.

The following example is a simple illustration of self-analysis, involving comparison of a person's view of himself with those of a number of close acquaintances. The individual concerned was asked to:

- describe what he saw as his main characteristics;
- ask a number of people who know him well but in different relation-ships to do the same thing;
- carry out an analysis of the views, asking:
  - How far do the commentators agree or disagree?
  - Is there any broad consensus about certain characteristics?
  - How do the views of the commentators compare with the views of the individual himself?

Individual's View of Self

Intelligent; conscientious; considerate; caring; sensitive; good sense of humour; articulate; witty; careless about minor details; impatient; easily roused to anger; very upset by any injustice.

Wife's View

Clever, sometimes too clever; hard-working; perfectionist; long-winded; very good memory for facts, but otherwise absent-minded; very dry sense of humour; moods vary between high and low; worries too much; has moments of self-doubt unnecessarily; very sensitive and thin-skinned; likes to be praised, but gets very upset by criticism; strong sense of justice; can be stubborn; generally thinks he is right, but is prepared to concede; inclined to be careless about dress; sometimes loses patience easily.

Sister's View

Clever; reliable; considerate; just and fair; tends to fuss and worry, often unnecessarily; has little concern for materialistic things; can be stubborn and likes to have his own way; a skilled talker and conversationalist; good sense of humour.

Work-colleague's View

Very capable, good with people, hard-working and very conscientious, inclined to worry and fuss if things are not 'as they should be'; sets self and others very high standards; gets 'bees in his bonnet'; sometimes surprisingly indecisive; gets very upset by criticism considered to be unfair; very dry sense of humour not always apparent to others; fluent writer and speaker; persuasive.

Secretary's View

Intelligent; friendly and approachable; considerate of others; insists on absolute accuracy; checks everything; talks a lot but has moods of silence; absent-minded; endless patience, tends to worry if things are not as he thinks they ought to be.

Friend's View

Very alert mind; sociable with very good sense of humour; considerate of others; very reliable; has wide range of interests; an interesting and amusing conversationalist; sometimes takes himself and life too seriously – a paradox; moods can fluctuate between jocular and morose; a complex personality – not easy to unravel.

Analysis of Commentator's Views

There is a broad consensus about plus and minus points:

(a) plus points· intelligent; conscientious; sensitive and caring; good sense of humour; sociable and good conversationalist;
(b) minus points: worries and fusses excessively; moods fluctuate; too thin-skinned; absent-minded.

Comparison of Other Views with Own Views

In the main, there is a general agreement between the two sets of views. The main points made by others, but not by the individual himself, are: excessive worrying; perfectionist approach to life; fluctuations of moods. There is complete disagreement on one point. He and his wife see impatience as a fault. His secretary, on the other hand, sees his 'endless patience' as a virtue. Nobody else comments on impatience, which seems therefore to be confined to the home and not to affect others.

(3) GROUPS AND LEADERSHIP

Groups

Clearly, an understanding of group dynamics and leadership is very important to managers when leading work-groups. Human beings are social creatures. As we have seen earlier, being in the company of others is one of the motivational benefits from membership of a work-group. At the same time, social relationships with others, as we all know, may produce conflicts within a group or between one group and another. The problem is endemic in human life. In the work situation, the successful performance of the group requires that individual energies should be directed towards the achievement of group goals and not dissipated by conflict. Effective performance of work by a group requires collaboration and harmony. It also requires compromise. Each member of the group will have differing motivational objectives, but these may need to be modified and subordinated to the common good.

One of the manager's primary tasks is to weld a number of individuals with different abilities, attitudes, values, interests, perceptions and needs into cohesive productive teams. Managers cannot please everybody and to attempt to do so will certainly result in failure. Considerable skill is needed in giving the group a sense of purpose so that if some individual needs are inevitably not satisfied, at least the group as a whole finds satisfaction and pride in the achievement of the team.

Close observation of groups in action has revealed the following phenomena of which managers need to be constantly aware in their roles as group-leaders.

1. **General effects of group membership**

    Membership of groups clearly affects individual behaviour. Influenced by other group members, individuals could, for example, be more forceful or submissive than they might otherwise be. The individual who might be a coward by himself, could display unchracteristic aggression or bravado as a member of a street gang. Spectators at football matches would be far less likely to hurl abuse at referees if they were watching the game alone. Put them in a crowd with hundreds of other people and behaviour can change dramatically. Their own wives and mothers might not recognize them.

    Membership of groups may have advantages and disadvantages for individuals in terms of the satisfaction or disappointment of their needs. On the one hand, they may benefit from feelings of security, of being useful, valued and esteemed by colleagues. They may satisfy needs for self-fulfilment and achievement as a result of collaboration with others. Only two of the mountaineering team that conquered Mount Everest in 1953 actually reached the summit, but the whole team bathed in the glory of the achievement. On the other hand, group membership may have adverse effects for individuals. If they have difficulty in relating to colleagues or experience any form of hostility, they are obviously likely to have feelings of insecurity, anxiety, frustration and low esteem. The kind of stress that people may experience through group membership in family, social or working life is something of which most people are aware. Adverse effects of living and working in groups must, of course, be seen in perspective. Individuals themselves must sometimes bear some responsibility for their own discomfort. We probably all know people whose psychological 'hang-ups' are such that they would always find it difficult to relate successfully with the other members of any group to which they may belong.

2. **Group norms**

   As the terms suggests, norms are the standards and characteristics of behaviour that particular groups may develop and exhibit. They could be described almost as rules of club-membership, which are not explicit, and of which the members are not overtly aware. They might show themselves, for example, in manners of speech, humour, group-jokes, attitudes and stereotypes. Those who accept and conform to the group norms are regarded as 'one of us'. Those who do not, are seen as outsiders, loners or mavericks. To illustrate with some examples, the norms of one well-known social group apparently requires its members to dye the hair red, green or blue, to wear rings through the ears or even the nose, and to wear faded and torn jean-trousers. The norms for another group, equally evidently, require wearing dark suits, bowler hats, club ties, carrying umbrellas, irrespective of the weather, and reading *The Times* newspaper. Norms in work groups could be regarded as no more than something of passing interest or a source of amusement. However, they could sometimes affect the individual's feelings of comfort or discomfort within the group. These feelings are especially relevant during the induction phase of employment, as we shall see later.

3. **Factions**

   The dictionary defines a faction as a party within a party, combined to promote their own interests, views or purposes at the expense of order and the public good. The development of splinter groups within groups is obviously not a healthy phenomenon, but it is a fact of organizational life that has to be recognized, discouraged and prevented by group leaders. It may affect all levels of organizations.

4. **Unofficial leaders**

   This aspect of group behaviour is obviously linked with intra-group factions. In any group, some personalities will always be stronger than others. These people are likely to represent any sub-groups that may form. As leaders of factions with an axe to grind, unofficial leaders may pose a threat to the authority of appointed leaders and to the collaborative efforts of the whole. The efforts of unofficial leaders are not necessarily always mutinous. They may sometimes be constructive, directed towards the achievement of group goals and intended to draw the manager's attention to things of which he or she needs to be made aware. However, this should not be necessary if managers have their eyes and ears open, are close to the group and know what is going on. In extreme cases, such as the Caine mutiny, for example, an unofficial leader might be necessary and justifiable in order to rescue the team from the consequences of a totally incompetent and unbalanced official leader.

5. **Inter-group conflict**

    This is often popularly described as a 'them and us' situation. Competition between various groups within an organization may sometimes be described as healthy or as friendly rivalry. If the competition is directed towards the common good of the organization as a whole, then no harm is done. Each group acknowledges the worth of the others. As most of us know from experience, inter-group rivalry can also be negative and destructive. Energy that should be directed towards achieving organizational goals is wasted in squabbling for resources or for purposes of prestige. Even in time of war, the main branches of armed forces have been known to waste valuable time and energy in attempting to spike each other's guns instead of those of the common foe. Bad leaders may foster group solidarity by developing hostile feelings towards other groups in the same organization. Good leaders act as links between one group and others in order to further the purposes and welfare of the organization as a whole.

6. **Pressure for conformity**

    This is a particularly interesting phenomenon of group behaviour, especially since pressure of this kind is not always overtly applied, but may be a subtle influence. Pressure by a majority or by a powerful element to coerce a minority to conform to societal norms has always been a feature of human life. Notwithstanding Margaret Thatcher's denial of the concept of society, social pressures provide demonstrable evidence that society, as an influencing force at least, does exist. The emergence of the so-called permissive society is another way of saying that previous societal pressures on people not to divorce, commit adultery or to produce illegitimate children have now been relaxed.

Similar pressures occur within work-groups by managers and a majority of group-members to persuade or coerce others to toe the line. The pursuit of group solidarity and pressures that may be applied to nonconformists has been the subject of a special study by Irving Janis, a social psychologist. He has coined the term 'group think' to describe the phenomenon. The summary of his conclusions are these:

(a) Groups, influenced by their leaders, naturally seek solidarity and avoidance of disruptive influences.

(b) Pursuing cohesiveness, groups tend to be uncritical of their own behaviour. (Examples of this tendency are regularly seen when a member of a governmental Cabinet makes a fatuous remark such as 'the British system of justice, education, health-care, etc. is the envy of the world'.)

(c) The tendency to close ranks can have serious consequences when important decisions are being taken. The lone, dissenting voice may have something significant to say. It could make the rest of the group examine alternative proposals and perhaps avoid taking a bad decision, which might result from the pursuit of consensus at all costs. Unfortunately, the lone dissenter tends to be overruled by the majority, who are not necessarily right.

These conclusions have important implications for management style and the process of decision-making. They imply that effective managers create an open atmosphere in which people are not frightened to say what they truly feel, even if they are in a minority. Peter Drucker, a well-known consultant and author on management subjects, has said that sound decisions need conflicting opinions. Managers should be very suspicious of immediate consensus. If this should happen, it is quite likely that they and the group-members have not thoroughly explored the arguments for and against a proposal, and especially the arguments against.

Leadership

Groups and leadership are complementary studies. All groups formed to achieve specific purposes need leadership, whether this role is fulfilled by an official or unofficial leader, or by several leaders. Somebody has to point the group in the right direction, see that it remains on course and that it achieves its goals. A significant consequence of the development of a complex, industrial society throughout the twentieth century has been the need for far more people to assume leadership roles than at any other time in human history. To make matters even more difficult, today's leaders function in a much more complicated world than those of bygone eras. In the past, leaders were mainly royal, noble, religious or political. The accepted style was universally authoritarian. Today's leaders have to operate with groups where expectations of members are very different and where the tasks to be performed are much more complicated. In former times leadership would not have been regarded as a subject for detailed and continuous study. In the modern world, understanding leadership, its nature and problems, and the requirements for effective practice are essential.

The study of leadership has gone hand-in-hand with the study of group behaviour. Leaders are also members of groups, influencing them and being influenced by them. They occupy a key position in the communication system.

As might be expected, studies of leadership have been principally concerned with leadership styles and the comparative efficacy of each. From the mass of research of data, the following generally agreed conclusions can be distilled:

1. Leadership styles range between two extremes – authoritarian and democratic-participative. The terms are self-explanatory. Authoritarian leaders tell and give orders; democratic-participative leaders consult team members and are more open to influence.
2. There is no one correct style. Various styles are appropriate to particular situations. For example, in a crisis the Chief of the Fire Brigade does not call all the team members together for a debate about what the best course of action might be. He has to be decisive and give orders. When long-term plans for the future are under consideration, managers would benefit from discussing questions with the team members, who will be affected by whatever is decided. Be that as it may; for reasons of personality, leaders tend to have preferred styles. The effective leader is the person who is able to judge the needs of varying situations and can be sufficiently adaptable and flexible to apply whatever style is appropriate.
3. The management of work groups requires attention to three areas – the task, the team, and the individual group members, the details of which are described below.

TASK

- Defining what has to be done and, in particular, identifying the overall aim, objectives, key-tasks and priorities.
- Deciding who is best suited to carry out what tasks.
- Ensuring that each team member knows and accepts what is required of him/her and what standards of performance are expected.
- Deciding what resources are needed and how they should be best allocated and most cost-effectively used.
- Deciding what methods are most likely to enable the aim and objectives to be reached.
- In practice, managing time and allocated resources as efficiently as possible to reach the aim and objectives.

THE TEAM

- Building and maintaining a cohesive, collaborative, productive unit.
- Building and maintaining harmonious links with other groups inside and outside the organization.
- Eliminating any destructive intra- or inter-group conflict.
- Maintaining discipline.
- Representing the team to higher authority and to peer groups inside and outside the organization.

INDIVIDUALS

- Knowing the individual members of the group.
- Being sensitive to individual strengths and weaknesses; needs for personal development.
- Being available to support, help, advise and encourage.
- Helping individuals to appraise performance by giving feedback and recognition (motivating).
- Developing individuals by delegating, broadening work experience, coaching and training.
- Attending to rewards, welfare, health and safety.
- Maintaining discipline.

Theory X and Theory Y

Of all the very many ideas that have been published about managerial styles throughout the past fifty years or so, probably the best known and the most influential are those expressed by Douglas McGregor in his classic *The Human Side of Enterprise*. In this book he describes two contrasting styles and approaches to the manager-leader role, which he calls Theory X and Theory Y. Theory X managers have a pessimistic view of human nature. They believe that the best results are achieved by carrot-and-stick methods. They are single-mindedly concerned with the task and production. Theory Y managers believe that since results depend mainly on the efforts and commitment of people, they must be given the highest priority. In consequence, the Theory Y manager adopts an open, participative style and attaches special importance to the development of his or her employees.

Considerable research into the effects of managerial styles on productivity have shown that, in general, a Theory Y approach has been and is more effective in motivating people in achieving group and organizational goals.

The quest for effectiveness as a manager-leader could be described as a never-ending pursuit of excellence – the pot of gold at the rainbow's end. We need to set ourselves the highest possible standards as a goal to be constantly pursued and as criteria for assessing our own performance and progress. How might the characteristics of the ideal manager-leader be described? The weight of evidence provided by studies of leadership over many years, from questionnaires answered by people attending management training courses from all parts of the world, and by the author's own long experience, suggest the following characteristics as leading candidates for inclusion in the list. Effective manager-leaders

1. are constant learners. They appreciate how difficult the manager's job is, especially in its human aspects. At the same time they also recognize its crucial importance. Therefore, they approach the job with humility and are always seeking to improve their own levels of knowledge, skills and performance;
2. have a good basic knowledge of human behaviour – of individual differences and their effects, of group behaviour, and of the requirements for effective leadership;
3. are good communicators. They are aware of the kinds of problems that regularly arise in the communication process, what the causes are, and how they may be anticipated and mitigated;
4. have a high level of interpersonal skills, developed by experience and training. They ask relevant questions and are good listeners. They

command interest and attention when speaking in public. They are effective leaders when conducting meetings;

5. set a good example to the members of their work-groups and so command respect. Being on top of their jobs in terms of professional competence, their approach to work and life is a model for the team to follow. They are infectiously enthusiastic, conscientious, inspiring and motivating. They do not have one set of standards for their own behaviour and another for the group-members;

6. do not act as though they have been appointed to manage by divine right. They are aware that the role is a temporary mandate, and that it does not imply that they are superior to the group members as human beings. They relate to other members on an adult–adult basis;

7. are fair, firm and consistent. They treat all members of the group similarly and do not reveal any personal likes and dislikes. They do not have favourites or *bêtes noires*. People know where they stand and are not subjected to fluctuations of moods, whims or caprices. They do not shirk being tough when the situation demands such action, e.g. when a member of the group steps out of line or does anything that detracts from the cohesion, performance and achievement of the group;

8. realize the importance of sound judgements to managerial effectiveness. They are aware of the problems of judgement and of what they need to do to make their judgements as sound as possible;

9. get out and about. This has been described as the GOYA approach. It has nothing to do with the Spanish artist of that name. It is an acronym for 'Get Off Your----' They have their eyes and ears open. Regularly moving amongst the members of their groups, they know what is going on. They are not the last to know if 'there is trouble at t'mill';

10. work in close collaboration with the group. They recognize that within the group there is likely to be considerable individual and collective talent available to help them in dealing with the problems they have to solve and the decisions they have to make, especially when the consequences directly affect the work and conditions of the group. They share information with the group to keep them in the picture and to avoid the spread of baseless rumours;

11. encourage and create an open, relaxed atmosphere. In this way, people are not frightened of the manager, nor to say honestly what they think and feel. Indeed they are encouraged to do so;

12. are in close contact with each individual member of their work-groups and
    (a) make quite sure that they fully understand what they are required to do,
    (b) involve them in a regular joint-participative appraisal of performance,
    (c) take a personal interest in them as people, attending to their welfare, being aware of their interests, skills and talents inside and outside of work, and of any personal problems that could affect work and for which help might be needed;
13. are approachable. Because of the relaxed, informal, open atmosphere created by the manager, members of the work group feel free to seek advice and help when they feel they need it. This is sometimes described as an 'open door' style of management. This in no way implies that people can walk into the manager's office as and when they feel like it, and expect immediate attention. Managers are very busy people. They also have a responsibility to other members of the group. They will respond to those seeking attention when they are free to do so. Moreover, they cannot waste time wet-nursing or spoon-feeding any weaklings there may be, who are for ever seeking shoulders to cry on;
14. give a very high priority to the development and training of the members of their groups. They have a good knowledge of the methods by which these purposes may be achieved. They also have acquired the necessary skills themselves to put this knowledge into effective practice. They liaise closely and co-operatively with the organization's training specialists in planning and providing cost-effective training and assessing its impact on work-performance;
15. discourage negative, destructive conflict. Conflict may occur within a group or between one group and another. Being primarily concerned with productive, effective work and performance, effective managers are alert to such contingencies and take steps to deal with such problems before they get out of control;
16. are good representatives of their groups. Managers represent their groups in relationship with higher authority and with other groups. Effective managers stand up for their groups. They represent accurately the group's feelings. They argue convincingly and strongly if need be to obtain resources or changes that the group may need. They show moral courage whenever this is necessary. They do not meekly surrender to higher authority on important issues, if they feel that

their own views and those of their groups should be strongly represented;

17. have a good sense of humour. Serious in their approach to the job, they are still able to see the funny side and do not get things out of proportion;

18. realize that they cannot please everyone in the group all the time. Nor should they try to do so. Some managers cannot comfortably assume the leadership mantle. They still want to be what is known as 'one of the boys' or 'popularity Jack'. Behaviour of this kind inevitably leads to a lack of respect and can cause all sorts of interpersonal problems, especially in disciplinary situations.

EXERCISE ON THE ANALYSIS OF MOTIVATION

1. Get the members of your work-group to complete the exercise.
2. Study the results and consider what they imply.
3. Discuss the results individually and collectively.
4. Carry out any action that seems necessary and practicable.

Task: Think about your working life very carefully and complete the two lists A and B described below on the separate form provided.

List A: In this column write down everything you can think of that you regard as important in your work in encouraging you to produce your best efforts and to provide satisfaction (motivating influences).

List B: In this column write down everything that has the opposite effect, i.e. discourages you from wanting to work enthusiastically, diminishes your interest, etc. (demotivating influences).

Note: When you have completed your lists, place a number against each item in order of its priority and importance, i.e. No. 1 in Column A means that this is the most important feature of work in providing encouragement and satisfaction. No. 1 in Column B means that this is the feature of work that discourages and dissatisfies you more than anything else. If some items are equal in importance give them the same number, i.e. if something is equally important to another in giving you maximum encouragement or satisfaction, then given them both a number one.

* Name ....

List A (Motivating influences)	No.	List B (Demotivating influences)	No.

---

* The exercise may be carried out anonymously, if the manager or trainer prefers.

NOTES ON EXERCISE ON ANALYSIS OF MOTIVATION

People naturally have differing, personal priorities that affect motivation. However, considerable research into the subject has produced conclusive evidence that people are not motivated to work mainly or solely for material rewards. Obviously, these are very important to employees, as industrial disputes over pay regularly show, but these are issues between senior, central, controlling management and the work-force as a whole. As far as relationships between junior managers and their work-groups are concerned, research indicates that people also attach particular importance to the following as motivating or demotivating factors:

- leadership style;
- job satisfaction;
- relationships with colleagues;
- recognition of contributions;
- help and advice;
- opportunities for development and advancement;
- fairness of treatment.

EXERCISE ON SELF-AWARENESS

- Refer to the example of self-analysis in this chapter.
- Use this as a model to produce a similar list of traits that you think best describe your personality. Include plus and minus traits.
- Ask a number of people who know you well in different situations to describe you in the same way, e.g. close relatives, friends, work colleagues, etc. Impress on them that their views must be as honest as they can be, otherwise the usefulness of the exercise is considerably diminished.
- Compare these views with your own, noting similarities and differences. Where there is a consensus of views, does this agree with your own view of self? If the consensus does not match your own view of self, what is your reaction to this divergence? Why do you think the difference of views exists?

EXERCISE ON LEADERSHIP

- Drawing upon your personal work experience, think of two managers whom you know well, one of whom you would describe as good and the other as bad in terms of their leadership and interpersonal behaviour.
- List the reasons why you rate one as good and the other as bad.
- Refer to the list of characteristics of effective manager-leaders in this chapter (pages 17–20). How does your good manager-leader compare with this list?
- How would you say your own performance compares with this list? In particular, are there any areas in which you think you might perform better?
- Are there any other characteristics not included in this list that you would include?

CHAPTER 2

Communication

BASIC QUESTIONS

1 What does the process of communication involve?
2 What is its importance in management?
3 What problems in communication regularly occur?
4 What are the causes?
5 How might they be mitigated or remedied?

Carl Duerr, a management consultant writing on the skills of management, has said: 'If I have to choose one word, then the one I would pick is communication. The single one thing that sorts out successes from failures is the ability to communicate with others. Your true managers are catalysts. They only succeed in that role if they effectively inform, instruct, persuade and motivate other people.'

Managers occupy a key position in the communication system. They are at the hub of the communication wheel from which messages flow inwards and outwards. Managers are the only members of work-groups with whom every other member has to communicate regularly. In addition to the hub-role within a particular work-group, managers are also the communicational links with other groups in the organization, with central, directing managers, and with external centres and agencies.

Communication is obviously of vital importance to effective management and hence to organizational success. At the same time, it is the source of abiding problems and a root cause of very many human difficulties. Failure to communicate bedevils human relationships of all kinds between nations, between and within political parties, between managers, unions and employees, between relatives, neighbours, etc.

In the light of such a widespread and continuing human problem, what can managers do to become effective communicators? First, they need to understand the essential nature of the process, its problems, causes and possible remedies. On the basis of this knowledge they can begin to develop the interpersonal skills that are needed for effective practice.

The Nature of the Communication Process

Human communication is a two-way activity. There is a sender and a receiver. The message has to be received and understood as intended, otherwise there is no communication. Because of traditional views of managers in an authoritarian role, they have tended to be seen as people who tell others what to do. In fact, the manager's job requires as much receiving as sending. Sound decisions must be based on sound information – what is known as intelligence in the military context. To be really effective they need to have skills in listening to other people's views, feelings and problems. We could perhaps describe the authoritarians as predominantly tellers and the democratic-participative managers as predominantly listeners.

The communication process is complex and subtle. It may take the following forms:

- spoken face-to-face;
- spoken at a distance (telephone);
- written;
- non-verbal.

The messages and the way they are interpreted are influenced by the individual characteristics and differences already discussed. As fundamental influences in the communication process they could be described as personal codes. Thus, A sends B a message in his or her code. It is interpreted in B's code. If the codes of A and B are significantly different, then communication may not be achieved. It could be said that A and B are 'not on the same wavelength' or 'do not speak the same language'. The biology of men and women is an example of a fundamental human difference that regularly leads to communication problems, sometimes with serious consequences.

Communication is affected by factors such as choice of words, which may well not have the same meaning for sender and receiver, position of words, emphasis, tone of voice, non-verbal signals, such as nods, winks, smiles, frowns, gestures and posture. Non-verbal behaviour and body-language have received considerable attention in recent times. No doubt it is important to be aware that people use methods other than words to convey their meanings. At the same time, it has to be realized that it is easy to misinterpret non-verbal signals. A frown may indicate disapproval, but also puzzlement. Non-verbal signals are not uniform in meaning. They are much affected by culture. Since many of us now live in multiracial societies, these variations need to be appreciated. The shaking of the head that means 'yes' in one country can mean 'no' in another. Two fingers may mean V for victory or something else. Messages that people send to one another may sometimes be affected by covert intentions, which senders may or may not realize at the conscious level. For example, the manager writing a report for the Managing Director may also be seeking, albeit subconsciously, to impress the recipient of the report with his or her knowledge, literary skills, intelligence and wit.

Problems of Communication

The root cause of problems of communication lies in individual differences and their effects on behaviour: this is an immutable fact of life. The kinds of problems that all of us experience at one time or another are caused by a failure to recognize these individual differences and to make allowances for them in relationships with others. How much easier life would be if others saw the world as we do? The inevitable egocentricity of the human condition makes it extremely difficult, if not impossible, to see the world from the point of view of other people. But this is what we must try to do if we are to communicate effectively. We all share common experiences such as hunger and thirst, but there are very wide differences in individual experiences. Those born into wealth and great comfort have no idea what it is like to be poor and hungry. When told that people were starving and had no bread, did Marie Antoinette really reply 'Why don't they eat cake?' The effects of differences in formative influences and the problems they may cause can be seen all the time in conflicts between parents and their offspring, because the societal norms are different for each. Immigrant families now settled in Britain may experience considerable difficulties of communication. For example, parents born and reared in India find it very difficult, if not impossible, to communicate with a daughter born and reared in Britain who wants to wear miniskirts, make-up, go to disco-clubs and stay out late.

Communicating Effectively

Effective communication begins with understanding the nature of the process, the effects on individual differences and the problems they cause. What might help managers to become effective communicators?

1. **Trying to anticipate and imagine – however difficult it may be – how others with whom they have to deal might think and feel**
   It requires a discipline – for discipline is what it is – to ask questions such as: 'How would I feel if somebody did or said that to me?' 'What effect is my proposed action likely to have on others?' 'If I make an ego-denting assault on the character of one of the members of my group, is that likely to change behaviour or would it make matters worse?' 'What do I really want to achieve?' 'Do I really want to change behaviour or do I simply want to blow my top?' 'If I really want to change behaviour, what is likely to be the best way?'

   Here we are talking about empathy and sensitivity. Examples of communicational errors caused by failures to think of the recipients' position abound in everyday life, e.g. the sales people or garrulous relatives and friends who telephone at very inconvenient moments and never bother to ask whether it is convenient to talk. The telephone can be a communicational curse. It allows people thoughtlessly to invade others' space without warning.

2. **Understanding and using the value of shared experience**
   Peter Drucker, a renowned commentator on management, has shrewdly observed that communication is based on shared experience. Because of individual uniqueness nobody can ever entirely share someone else's experience. As far as it is humanly possible, it evidently helps communication. When people live in two different worlds, like Marie Antoinette and the poor, destitute masses of eighteenth-century France, there is little hope of communication. In the world of work managers at all levels should do everything in their power to use the factor of shared experience in the cause of effective communication. Here are some real examples from organizational practice to illustrate the point:

   - In the police force everyone has to start on the bottom rung of the career path as a constable. In this way, those who reach the top of the ladder and become Chief Constables or Commissioners have served in every rank of the police force. They have not spent their careers in ivory towers. They know from personal experience what the constable's life is like and what it is like to arrest the drunk and disorderly on the streets of big cities in the small hours of Sunday morning. On all matters of police work they can truly communicate with all ranks of the force.

- Some years ago the Singapore government set up an induction training course for high fliers recruited to its Civil Service. These were graduates of exceptional potential ability, who were destined, barring unforeseen contingencies, to move rapidly to the top grades of the Civil Service. Bearing in mind the shared-experience factor, the course planners included regular attachments away from the classroom to various governmental offices. Here trainees worked for short periods carrying out the kinds of tasks that lower-grade staff had to perform, e.g. dealing face-to-face with difficult members of the public, carrying out a variety of menial and boring chores. When they reached the top of the career ladder, hopefully they would remember this experience and not make unreasonable demands of their staff.

- Medical students sometimes take holiday jobs as hospital porters or other low-grade jobs in and around the wards. When at some later date they become consultants, they may be better able as a result of this experience to empathize with those whose lot is to perform the dirty, unglamorous, but necessary tasks in hospitals.

- The last example concerns the central training institute of a very large organization. The training institute had two kinds of staff – managers and administrators, seconded from operational offices, and academic tutors recruited from universities, polytechnics, etc. employed on short-term contracts. The managers and administrative staff, being full-time employees of the organization, regularly complained that the academics were not in tune with the purposes, functions and culture of the employing organization. They were regarded as being 'a law unto themselves'. In consequence of these differing viewpoints communication problems regularly occurred. The answer lay in the hands of the employers. They should have:

  (a) arranged for the two groups to share work as much as possible so that working side by side each might stop stereotyping the other;
  (b) attached all newly appointed academic staff to work for short periods in operational offices before starting work at the training

institute, as a condition of employment. In this way, the academic tutors would have gained valuable firsthand knowledge of
the work of the employing organization and would, to some
extent at least, have shared experience with their managerial and
administrative colleagues. Since they were employed to train
staff from the operational offices of the organization, this policy
would have had a further invaluable communicational benefit.
The academic tutors would have had a much better knowledge
of the working lives of their trainees and in consequence would
have been able to relate to them with a much greater
understanding.

Sharing experience is the antidote to stereotyping – a common
communicational problem. People take up entrenched positions.
They put others in categories and 'tar them all with the same
brush'. It leads to unwarranted and sometimes dangerous
beliefs: e.g. Scots are mean; young people are irresponsible;
women are not as good drivers as men. The award-winning TV
film *Prime Suspect* illustrated the stereotyping and prejudices of a
group of male police officers towards their female manager.
Once they had shared the experience of working together to
solve a major crime, the stereotyping ceased and communication
was established.

3. **Choosing the right form of communication**
In the work situation we can communicate face-to-face, in writing or
by telephone. In some circumstances the mode of communication is
not particularly important: in others it most certainly is. The choice of
method will depend on purpose, but as a very general rule face-to-face
communication has particular advantages. The language is likely to be
less formal and stuffy than written communication. Questions can be
asked and understanding checked. Some managers, and especially
those who tend to isolate themselves from their groups, have a
penchant for sending memos, even though the recipients are in offices
only a few minutes' walk or less away from the manager's office.

There are, of course, some occasions when written communication
is obviously necessary. It may take the form of letters, minutes, formal
warnings of misconduct, etc. Because of the problem of human
subjectivity, it is very difficult for writers themselves to see anything in
their writings that might cause problems and misunderstandings, but
to avoid the ever-present chance of misunderstanding, it is very

helpful, if not to say necessary, to get somebody else to check what has been written. An objective viewpoint is needed.

4. **Choosing the right time**

   Choosing the right time to attempt to communicate with another person applies much more to spoken than to written communication. The right time means that the recipient is ready to listen. However impatient senders may be to say what they want to say, communication cannot be achieved with people who are preoccupied with other thoughts or activities. As always, effective communication requires sensitivity. We need to check whether the intended recipients are ready and prepared to listen. Here again the telephone can be a great nuisance, unless the caller asks whether it is convenient for the person receiving the call.

5. **Checking understanding**

   Breakdowns in communication regularly occur because neither A nor B realize that they have different perspectives and different interpretations of messages. It can happen that people become locked in conflict without realizing what the difference is really about or that sometimes there is no serious disagreement between them. This is why disinterested, third parties often play an important role in unravelling communicational knots. Not having an axe to grind, they can take an objective and independent view and see what the problem is and what needs to be done.

   Here are two examples of misjudgements that could occur from a failure to check understanding. Both are taken from selection interviews. Asked what his hobbies were, a candidate replied that he had none. In consequence, the board members gave him a low assessment because, apparently, he did nothing useful or interesting in his spare time. One of the board was not satisfied with the judgement and, as a result, the candidate was asked to return so that the matter could be settled. The question was put in a different form. The candidate was asked what he did in his spare time. This time the answer was very different. He produced a long list of interesting and worthwhile activities – sporting, social, cultural, travel, etc. The stumbling-block was the word 'hobbies' which the candidate understandably interpreted to mean activities like woodwork, stamp collecting, etc.

   In another selection interview, a candidate explained that he had left a job because of 'a difference over money'. Pressed to explain what this answer meant, the candidate revealed that some money was missing from the firm's petty cash-box and he was suspected of having taken it.

What might be described as an 'I think that you think' situation is a very common cause of communicational misunderstandings. Here is an example to show how lines of communication can become seriously distorted. A thinks that B dislikes him for some reason or other. B has never said at any time that she dislikes A, but apparently there is something in her demeanour that causes him to believe so. It also has to be said that there is something in A's personality – excessive sensitivity perhaps – that contributes to his feelings. In fact, B does not dislike A, and would be very surprised to know how he feels. This unwarranted and inaccurate assumption affects the way that A behaves towards B. She perceives A's demeanour as unnecessarily cold and somewhat aggressive. She reacts accordingly and so the communication breakdown goes on unrepaired. In the work situation, managers who are communicationally skilful can prevent problems such as this and the possibly serious consequences from arising. It is achieved by encouraging openness and persuading people to have trust and to lay their cards on the table. Initially, it does not matter whether people's feelings appear to be justified or unwarranted. It is not a question of 'I can't see why you should think that'. The fact is that, rightly or wrongly, what the other person thinks must first be listened to carefully. Only when true feelings are revealed can there be any attempt to unravel misunderstandings or to correct false assumptions and impressions.

6. **Reducing links in the chain**

   Communication is difficult enough between two people, but if a message is passed on by several people, there is every possible chance that they will add their own interpretations. By the time it reaches the end of the chain it might well be very different from the original message. Gossip and rumour are examples of the distorting process with which we are all familiar. They show what happens when a message passes from one person to another. Managers may tell their deputies that they are not too pleased about something or other. By the time this fairly mild comment has been passed around, it may well have been translated as 'the boss is hopping mad'. If the message is important and managers want to ensure that everyone from the higher to the lower levels receives the same unadulterated version, then they must communicate directly. They can do this in two ways, as they think best. They can write the message they wish to convey in clear, unequivocal language, get somebody else to check to ensure there is no chance of misunderstanding, and then send a copy to every member of the group. Alternatively, they can assemble all the members of the group for which they are responsible, tell them what they want to say, and then ask if anyone wishes to raise any questions. Speaking directly to the troops was a form of communication that General Montgomery demonstrated to be very effective. As a corollary, it is worth mentioning that managers need to be always alive to the effects of rumour and the serious consequences it may sometimes have. Clearly they cannot control the ways in which others may distort their remarks. Knowing, however, how easily this can happen they need to be careful in making chance remarks about any subject that is important to the work group. They also need to keep their staff fully informed about everything that concerns them so as to avoid festering and morale-sapping rumours.

7. **Developing listening skills**

Because of the inevitable egocentricity of human nature, listening in the truest sense is something that humans in general find difficult to do. It is a very important part of the communication process and a fundamental skill in effective management. Because of its importance it will be discussed in depth in Chapter 3, Interpersonal Skills.

Because communication is always affected by factors such as individual differences in life's experience and formative influences, there are no easy answers to problems of human communication that textbooks or training courses could provide. In practice, effective communication requires a desire to communicate and considerable effort. It requires personal discipline, the ability to empathize with others, endless patience and tolerance. These qualities are best developed early in life by an enlightened education system that places at least as high a value on human relationships and interpersonal skills as it does on the acquisition of knowledge.

EXERCISE ON COMMUNICATION

- Drawing on your own experience of work and of life in general, describe any examples of communicational problems that you can recall.
- Analyse what you consider to be the causes of these problems.
- How might they have been prevented or mitigated?

CHAPTER 3

Interpersonal Skills

BASIC QUESTIONS

1 What is the importance of skills of asking and listening in management?
2 What are the essential features of an effective questioning technique?
3 What does listening really mean? How does it differ from hearing?
4 What are the common barriers to effective listening?
5 Can listening skills be developed, and if so how?
6 Why are speaking skills important to managers?
7 What are the factors that determine effectiveness of speaking: (a) in general (b) in detail?
8 What purposes might meetings and discussions serve?
9 How does a knowledge of individual and group behaviour assist those who lead meetings and discussions?
10 What is required of those who chair meetings to ensure effectiveness?

(1) ASKING AND LISTENING

Human beings are generally predisposed more to talking and telling than to asking and listening. The educational system tends to emphasize skills such as reading, writing and speaking. It is only comparatively recently that listening has been recognized as a very important communicational skill and included in management training courses. Traditionally, people in positions of authority are seen as those who know the answers, who tell, persuade and convince others. Anyone with experience of teaching people from certain so-called developing countries will know that the tradition dies hard. Some students from these parts are often not used to teachers who ask them what they think. Teachers are supposed to know and tell.

Evidence of a lack of skills in asking and listening is all around us. A group of politicians from different parties debating issues on television can be relied upon to trot out the same old clichés, paying no heed to what others are saying, doing far more telling than asking and listening. It is not unusual for such discussions to become chaotic with everyone talking at the same time. The same behaviour and deficiencies can be observed at social events, such as cocktail parties and family gatherings. Dale Carnegie made a fortune in pursuing the theme in his famous book *How to Win Friends and Influence People*.

Skills in asking and listening are extremely important to effectiveness in management. They are an essential part of the armoury of the democratic-participative, Theory Y manager.

Asking

Asking questions is crucial to scientific discovery and philosophical inquiry: Why do apples fall to the ground? What is knowledge? How did the universe begin? Management could be described as a process of asking the right questions as an essential prerequisite to finding the right answers: What questions should we be asking? What do we want to achieve? What would be the best way to achieve the aim?

Questioning skills are needed at every turn in the process of management, e.g. gathering information as a basis for making decisions, chairing meetings and discussions, conducting selection interviews, performance appraisal, tutoring in training courses, counselling, disciplinary inquiries, etc. The skills such as those needed for the purposes of effective management are not developed simply by the experience of everyday relationships. They need to be learned through training. The main problem that nearly all untrained questioners have is the inability to approach the task with an open mind. It needs awareness of the problem and discipline to curb and eradicate natural tendencies to make assumptions about others. However, once aware of what is required, all the evidence indicates that, with training and practice, managers can acquire the necessary questioning skills. The main general requirements are these. As a general rule, questions should:

1. **Be simple**. For example 'What do you think we should do?' Some questions could hardly be recognized as questions. They are reminiscent of the kinds of questions sometimes set in examination papers. A fairly long statement is made, which ends with the word 'discuss'.

2. **Be open**. Open questions are those which are free from any bias, or influence or suggestion of answers on the part of the questioners. In legal terms, they are not leading questions. Rudyard Kipling made the point about the potential benefits of open questions in the couplet: 'I keep six honest serving-men/(They taught me all I knew)/Their names are What and Why and When/And How and Where and Who.' Open questions begin with interrogative words such as these. They cannot be answered by yes or no. They are the most productive of information and the most likely to reveal the truth. Here is an example to show how one open question leads to another:

Question: Why did you leave the job?
Answer: Because I was bored.
Question: Why were you bored?
Answer: Because the job did not offer me the kind of challenge I was looking for.
Question: What sort of challenge were you looking for? and so on.

Pursuing this line of inquiry, questioners learn much more than mere facts. They learn what lies behind them. In the example given above, questioners could learn something useful about people being interviewed – what motivates them, what demotivates.

To ask, for example: 'Did you feel annoyed when that happened?' suggests the possibility of annoyance. A much better form would be: 'How did you feel when that happened?'

Questioners do not need slavishly to use the open form for every single question. There are occasions when a yes-no answer is needed, e.g.: 'Was it single-sex or mixed school?'

The open forms of questioning are not only a matter of effective technique. It has much to do with the questioner's attitude and with the importance of approaching questioning with an open mind. A question that begins with: 'I suppose you . . . ' is not really a question at all. It is an expression of an unwarranted assumption.

3. **Not supply answers**. Sometimes a good open question is spoiled because the questioner supplies the answer, e.g.: 'Why did you leave the job? Was it because you were looking for better paid employment? Some questioners are unable to ask a question and then wait for the

answer. Sometimes a period of silence has to be tolerated whilst the person being questioned thinks about the reply.

4. **Be asked one at a time**. A common fault with untrained questioners is to ask a number of questions all at the same time. For example, 'When did you first hear about your promotion? Were you excited? What did your family say? Does it mean that you will have to move?' How can anybody be expected to cope adequately with four questions all at once.

5. **Put information in perspective**. If somebody tells a questioner that he or she came third in a race, it would be useful to know how many people took part in the race before offering any congratulations for athletic prowess. If the answer to the follow-up question were three, any initial assumption would need to be revised.

6. **Be pertinent and likely to produce required and valuable information**. For example: 'Why do we do it this way? What would happen if we . . . ? What do you think the problem is? What do you think we should do?

   A managerial questioning technique that has been proved to be very effective in practice is to ask the same question of a number of people. If there is a consensus, managers should give the agreed answer serious consideration as a basis for action, but not inevitably so. If there is disagreement, then obviously they need to do some further research before taking action. Incidentally, it is interesting to note the disagreement that regularly occurs when experts are asked the same question.

Listening

Listen and learn is sound proverbial advice, but difficult to achieve in practice. As we have already seen, the central problem lies in human egocentricity and the individual differences that always complicate the process of communication. Because it is now recognized, much more than ever before, that listening is an essential skill for effective management, it has been the subject of research and is often included in courses of training in management and related subjects. Some of the evidence of research made depressing reading about the low levels of listening ability and skills that most of us have.

Arising from the central problem, a number of common barriers to effective listening have been identified, such as:

- not concentrating and being distracted by other things competing for attention;

- allowing prejudices, assumptions, emotions, etc., to distort messages;
- 'switching off' when people whom we dislike, or with whom we regularly disagree, are speaking;
- making hasty judgements and not hearing speakers out;
- interrupting before others have finished saying what they wish;
- waiting impatiently to get a word in and thinking more about this than what the speaker is saying.

No doubt all of these faults regularly occur. But what is to be done? In practice, it is hardly likely to be of much use to make managers aware of the faults and then issue a list of 'I must nots'. There is no reason why we should pay attention to some ranting or boring speaker. If speakers send us to sleep, the fault is as much or more theirs than ours. Too many textbooks on the subject are long on theory but short on advice that could be effective in practice. How well or badly people listen in their spare time is their business. What is certain, however, is that managers must develop listening skills as an essential factor in effective management. So what can they do to develop these important and necessary skills?

1. Give the speaker full attention and above all maintain eye contact. Do not engage in distracting activities, e.g. rummaging through drawers, polishing fingernails, writing, wandering around the room, etc.
2. Intervene only at appropriate moments to ask short, simple, open questions, e.g. 'So what did you decide to do?'
3. Use the eyes as well as the ears to pick up non-verbal clues.
4. Tolerate silence. When the speaker pauses to reflect, it is not essential for the listener to fill the gap.
5. Check understanding as necessary, e.g. 'Have I understood you correctly?' 'You seem to be saying . . .' 'When you say . . . what exactly do you mean?'
6. Get feedback on behaviour. The importance of self-awareness has already been emphasized in Chapter 1 (2). It may cause some discomfort to have our weaknesses pointed out, but there is no better way than asking people who know us really well to tell us the truth as they see it. The research on listening, mentioned earlier, revealed that most people are not aware of their shortcomings and regularly overestimate their listening skills. It might come as a bit of a shock to be told: 'You tend to do all the talking. It's difficult to get a word in edgeways with you. You're always interrupting. You seldom let me finish what I want to say. With you things often go in one ear and out of the other', especially if several of our acquaintances make similar comments. It

may be hard to break the habits of a lifetime, but this is the start of the road to redemption.

7. Use discussions with staff to practise listening skills. Skilful listening is hard work. It requires continuous concentration, attention, sensitivity, patience, tolerance and discipline.

(2) SPEAKING TO GROUPS

Speaking to groups large and small is a skill that all managers need to have. They will certainly have to speak to their own work-groups from time to time. They may sometimes be required to address other managers within the employing organization, clients, customers or other external groups. At other times they may be required to contribute to training courses as speakers or tutors. The specific purposes of talks will naturally vary, but the general purposes are always the same – to inform or persuade, or both.

To be effective, speakers have to get their audiences on their side and avoid doing anything that could have the opposite effect. They need to arouse interest and attention, to achieve impact, to stimulate, to give people food for thought. When all is said and done, they need to persuade their audiences that what they have heard was well constructed, well presented and useful. The alternative is to switch off the audience's listening mechanisms, perhaps providing people with unintended opportunities to catch up on lost sleep, lulled by a boring voice delivering a boring subject.

This analysis in detail of the ingredients for success, hopefully will help to dispel beliefs, held by some that effective speaking depends much on nature's endowments, on having what is popularly known as 'the gift of the gab'. Undeniably, for reasons of personality some people have a start over others. Adolf Hitler owed much of his political success to an uncanny ability to hypnotize audiences. He was able to persuade them to forget the critical faculties that would otherwise have told them that he was talking dangerous nonsense. It is unlikely that he ever attended a course on public speaking.

All the same, ordinary mortals, who are often diffident about their oratorical potential and may dread the prospect of facing audiences, can take heart. There are numerous examples of distinguished speakers who have confessed to feelings of diffidence and anxiety, sometimes even when their reputations were well established. Winston Churchill, for example, acknowledged as a master of the art, apparently did not find public speaking easy at the start of his career. As with other human skills, people often have more potential than they realize. Practice may not in truth make perfect, but if the bases are sound, there is ample evidence that those whose performance was initially poor or moderate can achieve significant improvement over time. The factors that contribute to effectiveness in speaking in public are varied and numerous. If these are analysed systematically, two broad categories can be identified – what speakers need to consider and do before and during a talk. In short, it is a question of what you say and how you say it.

BEFORE THE TALK

There is a pertinent aphorism sometimes quoted by trainers on courses in public speaking: 'Fail to prepare, prepare to fail'. The importance of careful and thorough preparation for speaking to groups cannot be emphasized too strongly. People who have limited or no experience of public speaking probably cannot begin to imagine just how much attention needs to be given to preparation. On the day the speech may flow logically, coherently, convincingly and, perhaps, amusingly. It may give the impression that it is all happening naturally, spontaneously and effortlessly. Do not believe it. *Ars est celare artem*. The art lies in concealing the art.

Comprehensive preparation of a talk requires attention to details such as: purpose; title of talk; the audience; the contents; illustrative anecdotes; timing; dealing with questions; aids to speaking; and environmental details. These are now discussed in detail below.

Purpose

It is a managerial axiom that definition of purpose is the first essential for achieving a goal. Speakers should begin by being very clear in their minds precisely what they wish to achieve: to think about the needs of their audiences, asking what should the audience know by the end of the talk, how well would they be able to summarize what has been said.

Title of Talk

Definition of purpose and title are closely linked. The title should reflect what the talk intends to achieve and cover. A talk was recently described in an advertising brochure by a one-word title, i.e. 'Interviewing'. The title suggested a comprehensive coverage of the subject. In fact, it dealt with only one kind of interview – the selection of new employees. The kind of title that would have accurately reflected the speaker's intentions should have been expressed in some such terms as: 'Effective interviewing for selecting new employees'.

The Audience

Considering the audience is obviously of fundamental importance. Without the audience there is no reason for the talk to be given. How to get the required message across must be uppermost in speakers' minds. Speaking in public should not be an occasion for an ego-trip. Before planning the talk in detail, speakers need to give very careful thought to their audiences in terms of their backgrounds, their likely knowledge and experience, numbers attending, etc. The more information speakers can acquire about their audience the more likely it will be that they can adapt what they have to say to those who are going to listen to the talk.

Cultural differences are a regular source of problems to speakers. Considerable tact and sensitivity are essential. Educational, religious and work-practices may be very different from those to which the speakers are accustomed. Attempts at humour could misfire. In general, people are amused by much the same things all over the world, but the British irreverence towards higher authority, for example, is not readily appreciated in some eastern parts of the world.

We need to practise what we know about communicational skills, which are based on empathy, putting ourselves in others' shoes, asking: Who are they? What are they likely to know already? What do they want to know? What would be the most effective way of getting the message across? How might they react? What questions might they raise?

The Contents

In planning contents, speakers need to consider main headings, sub-headings, points to be covered and order of subjects. When this has been done, they can turn to issues such as illustrative anecdotes, timing, aids to speaking and environmental details, etc.

An old adage given as advice to trainee-speakers says: 'Begin by telling them what you are going to tell them; then tell them; finally, tell them what you have told them.' This is another way of saying that a well-planned talk has three discernible phases – a beginning, a middle and an end, i.e. an introduction, the main substance of the talk, and a conclusion.

Using the broad framework described above, speakers have to work out what topics will be included under each of the three headings and in what order. The items to be covered in the introductory phase will normally be the same for most talks, i.e. aim, objectives, scope of the talk, etc. When it comes to the main, central part of the talk, speakers need to consider what topics are relevant and what the logical order would be. A useful approach to this task is the brainstorming technique, i.e. to write down uncritically whatever ideas come into the head without bothering about relevance or order. The next stage is to go through these first notes, accepting and rejecting as appropriate. The final stage is to work out what seems to be the most logical order of topics. It is often helpful to express topics in the form of questions, as shown in the example of a plan for a talk at the end of this chapter.

Thinking of the plan in terms of questions tends to focus attention on what the right order ought to be. The concluding phase is a summary of the main points that have been covered.

Illustrative Anecdotes

The dictionary defines an anecdote as a short account of an incident. When used appropriately and with relevance, they can be extremely useful as a means of relating points made in a talk to reality. They help to bring particular points home to the audience in a colourful, interesting and impressive way. As they move through the list of topics, speakers should try to think of incidents that have occurred to illustrate particular points they wish to make. If the anecdotes are also humorous, so much the better.

Timing

How long should a talk last? The duration of a talk may be determined by several factors. Somebody else may decide the time to be allocated, as for example when a talk is part of a programme. The points that speakers want to cover is another possible determinant. Most important of all is the question of the limits of human endurance and concentration. There is no magic figure, but probably about one hour is about as much as most people can take at one sitting, even with the most accomplished and interesting speakers. If speakers need to speak longer than that, then they must give the audience a chance to stretch their legs for say fifteen to twenty minutes before continuing. Speakers who are fascinated by their own eloquence and become oblivious of time, are very likely to defeat their own purposes and to risk antagonizing the people who should be listening, co-operatively and sympathetically.

It is also very important to get the balance right in allocating time to each topic covered by the plan. This is not an easy task, but it should improve with practice. Some speakers never seem to learn. They look at the clock, see that little time is left and still much remaining that they wish to say. They are rushed for time and find themselves making apologies – an admission of bad time-managment that will lose marks with the audience.

Questions

Questions have an obvious bearing on timing. The wishes of members of audiences must also be met. Questions could be raised at any time during the talk or at the end. There is a potential problem if questions are taken during the talk itself: they could consume a fair amount of time, especially if the questioners are persistent, the questions complicated, and the speakers inordinately generous. The problem is even worse if the question is irrelevant or of interest only to the questioner. The matter needs skill and tact. Whatever speakers may feel, they must never show any signs of impatience or irritation.

Probably the most satisfactory solution is to take questions as they come and then decide whether they can be answered briefly or require more time. If they do need more time, they can be postponed until 'question time' at the end of the talk. At any time, when a question is raised which is of interest only to the questioner, the best response probably is to say something like: 'Thank you for your interesting question. However, since it only seems to affect you and may need further discussion, I suggest that we meet afterwards to discuss it together'. What could be more helpful or courteous than that?

Aids to Speaking

There is a wide range of aids available to speakers – *aide-memoire* notes, audi-visual media of various kinds and hand-out material. These are discussed separately in turn below.

1. **Aide-memoire notes**
   Speakers need to use some form of written material to remind them of the topics to be covered and in what order. There is a small minority

of speakers who prefer to speak extemporaneously. This is a *tour de force* which no doubt impresses a number of people. We sometimes hear people say admiringly: 'He/she spoke without notes.' Nevertheless, this can hardly be described as good practice, except perhaps for the light-hearted after-dinner speech. It is like walking along a high wire without a safety net. It is a needless risk. Even the most gifted are still human and fallible. They could easily miss an important point that needs to be covered. In moments of complete aberration they could even miss out a complete heading. At the other extreme some people, when making a formal speech, write out the text and then learn it by heart. This practice too has its disadvantages. It robs the speech of spontaneity that comes when speakers rely on the inspiration of the moment. But more than that – anything learned by heart, like the lines of a play, can be forgotten. So, if written material is to be used as an aid to speaking, speakers have two choices. They can either use a full text or brief notes.

Reading a prepared text is acceptable practice in certain circumstances. When speakers are making formal speeches from a platform at a distance from the audience and where eye-contact is not possible, a prepared text could be used. Even so, speakers still need to develop the skill to speak with unobtrusive glances down at the text. To speak, as some people do at political party and union conferences, with their eyes permanently fixed on a written text, is a certain way to lose all impact and interest.

The method that meets every situation, whether speakers are addressing large audiences or small groups, is to use brief headings to remind speakers of the topics to be covered and in which order. This method allows the best of both worlds. They know in advance what they are going to say, the notes provide an *aide-memoire*, and they can use the language and style they would use in ordinary conversation.

2. **Audio-visual media**

These include overhead-projector (OHP) transparencies, flip-charts, magnetic boards, slides, audio-tapes and films. If a period of about one hour is the accepted limit for the duration of a talk, then clearly there is a limit to the amount of time available for the use of some of these aids. If slides, tapes or films are to be included amongst the aids, they can only be used for very brief periods. Otherwise, they need to be used in a separate session. In practice, the most commonly used aids to illustrate talks are OHP transparencies and flip-charts. Their obvious advantages over the 'chalk and talk' method are these:

(a) they can be prepared in advance;

(b) speakers can continue speaking facing the audience. They do not have to interrupt the flow of speaking and turn their backs on the audience, whilst writing on the board;

(c) they can be used repeatedly;

(d) they can be used as the speaker's *aide-memoire* notes and at the same time provide signposts for the audience, so that they can more easily follow the direction of the talk;

(e) since the visual is a most powerful learning channel, they help the audience to concentrate and to keep the attention from wandering;

(f) OHP transparencies can be copied and used as hand-out material to remind members of the audience of the important topics and points covered in the talk.

The teaching points that are always made about the production of visual aids seem far too obvious to need mentioning. Nevertheless, experience shows that some speakers still fail to give proper attention to the production of visual-aid material. Neglect of this kind is another way in which speakers, no doubt unwittingly, can put the backs up of their audiences and irritate those whose attention they are trying to attract and sustain. Poor visual aids are likely to be seen as signs that speakers are incompetent or do not care about their audiences.

If supported by the resources of large organizations, speakers can usually obtain visual aids that are professionally produced. Whether they have these facilities or not, the following advice is universally applicable:

(a) Always begin by making a rough draft on paper.

(b) Amend and revise what has been written so that the message is economical with words, but at the same time conveys the required messages unambiguously and concisely.

(c) Make sure that the page is uncluttered and legible.

(d) Print the text and do not use cursive handwriting.

(e) Test the effectiveness of aids before using.

3. **Hand-out material**

Speakers cannot hope to cover all there is to say about a subject in the time normally available for a talk. There is an obvious caveat about handing out material of this kind during the talk. If speakers intend to talk about the contents of the hand-out, there is no problem. If, however, they intend members of the audience to read the material at a later time, they must not be surprised if people start to read there and then, and stop listening to what the speaker is saying. Unless the material is to be used as part of the talk, hand-out texts should be distributed at the end.

Environmental Details

It would be tedious to try to list every single thing that speakers need to consider. Only they know what should be checked, e.g.: Are the seating arrangements what they want? Is all the necessary equipment in place? Is it working? Are there any distractions, such as external noise? Are visual aids visible from the back of the room? and so on. Anyway, whatever the details may be, speakers should carry out a thorough check to see that everything is in order before they give a talk. Preparatory checks are especially important if the talk is being given in an unfamiliar environment. To walk into a strange room to give a talk, not having visited it beforehand, is asking for trouble. Meticulous attention to detail makes all the difference between success and failure. Speakers who leave everything to chance and rush breathlessly into the room with a few minutes to spare deserve all that they get. Unfortunately, it is their audiences who suffer from this indifference. Effective speakers care and prepare.

There is one final stage to the preparatory phase that needs to be discussed. Actors rehearse their plays before the actual performance. Speakers need to do the same. Going through the talk in this way is essential to see whether any amendments are necessary, e.g.: Has too much time been given to one topic and not enough to another? Does the visual material need to be changed? Since a second opinion is always very valuable, speakers can gain considerable help and also reassurance by rehearsing talks with a relative, friend or colleague. If help of this kind is not available, rehearsals can still and should be carried out by speakers alone.

DURING THE TALK

The meticulous attention to detail in the preparatory phase should already have set speakers well on the way to success. They still have the task of facing their audiences and communicating their messages convincingly. Unfortunately, human beings are prone to judge by appearances. All speakers, therefore, will inevitably be judged not only on what they say, but how they speak. Some speakers may prepare their material very carefully, but diminish its effect by a lack of presentational skills. Others may skimp the preparatory phase, but yet succeed in impressing their audiences with the brilliance of their oratorical abilities. Audiences are entertained, but not informed. Such speakers ramble without structure, perhaps talking nonsense, but presenting it very articulately.

Effective speakers are those who rate well on both counts. Analysing the elements that contribute to presentational skills, we need to consider such factors as control of nerves, demeanour, posture, gesture, voice and elocution, eye-contact, sensitivity to the audience, humour. These factors are inevitably linked to the physical characteristics and personalities of individuals. Some people have jolly, bubbling personalities; others are by nature less forward. A person who normally speaks with a quiet voice cannot be expected to acquire the power of an Italian tenor for the purposes of public speaking. We must make the best of what we have. We need to be well aware of human characteristics that can make or mar effectiveness in presenting a talk and know whether there is anything typical of our own behaviour that could adversely affect our performances. Because we cannot see ourselves as others see us, we need evidence to be fed back. This can be obtained either by videos or reports by observers.

The easiest way to obtain necessary feedback is to ask a friend or colleague to sit at the back of the room whilst the talk is being given, and to make notes for later discussion. Incidentally, it is very important that any report of this kind should include the plus points.

The following analysis of the factors that affect the effectiveness of presentation takes account of individual differences. It is not intended to propose uniform standards. Variety is the spice of life. It is concerned only with what can help and what can hinder the presentation of talks.

Control of Nerves

People attending training courses on presentational skills provide strong evidence that control of nerves and stage-fright is a major worry for inexperienced speakers. Some people can be paralysed with fear at the prospect of standing alone in front of an audience and feeling the laser-effect of numerous pairs of eyes focusing in their direction. Like so many other human problems they fail to realize that they are by no means unique in experiencing such feelings. Even very experienced speakers confess to some flutterings when faced with this task. The condition is usually at its worst just before rising to speak. Once the talk is launched, experienced speakers know that not only does the pain disappear, but they often begin to enjoy the occasion. There is no simple remedy. Certainly resort to alcohol or drugs is very likely to have results that could be disastrous. Speakers who do this may eliminate the immediate pain, but they run the risk of a disastrous presentation, that the members of the audience may remember for a long time to come for all the wrong reasons.

What help can be given to speakers on the subject of nerves?

1. **Remember that you are not as alone as you may think**. Unless you, the speaker, antagonize them because of poor preparation, audiences are mostly on your side. They do not on the whole enjoy your feelings of discomfort or embarrassment.

2. **Nerves are essential to success**. We need, so to speak, the adrenalin to flow. This is what sportsmen call being 'psyched-up'. These feelings that seem to inexperienced speakers like a disadvantage are, in fact, a potential advantage.

3. **Remember the maxim 'fail to prepare, prepare to fail'**. In the earlier part of this chapter the importance of preparation was very strongly emphasized and discussed in detail. The knowledge that you have prepared for your talk as thoroughly as possible is invaluable in the control of nerves. You have decided your destination and the route. You have anticipated any possible problems. In short, you know what you have to do and how you are going to do it. That in itself is a great comfort and an aid to confidence.

4. **Any experienced speaker will confirm that things get better with practice**. The feelings of some tension that arise when the adrenalin starts to flow seldom go away, but confidence grows with each successful talk. If something occurs, such as a temporary black-out, the experienced speaker will know that these things can happen – fortunately very rarely – and how to deal with the situation. The President of the Royal Academy, a distinguished public speaker, once dried up unexpectedly when addressing a large audience after dinner in the dining-room of a London Club. Instead of becoming confused and embarrassed, he simply said to the audience: 'I'm terribly sorry, ladies and gentlemen. I have completely forgotten what I wanted to say next. Would you please mind just talking amongst yourselves for a few moments whilst I recollect what I wanted to say'. Everybody laughed and the speaker was soon back on the rails once more.

Demeanour, Posture and Gesture

Here we are considering how speakers stand, move and deport themselves. Speakers' main concern should be to avoid anything that might distract their audiences. Excessive movement or repeated mannerisms should, therefore, be avoided. A film in the famous Sergeant Bilko series was based entirely on speakers' mannerisms. The colonel was at a loss to understand why Sergeant Bilko and his men, who normally spent all their spare time in money-making schemes and gambling, should be attending a series of lectures on the history of art in the camp's education centre. They did this because the lecturer had a very distinctive mannerism. The group would bet on how many times she scratched the back of her leg during each lecture.

At the other end of the scale some speakers are far too statuesque and wooden. Audiences are not inspired by zombies. They want to see signs of life, energy, enthusiasm and humour in speakers.

Voice and Elocution

It goes without saying that the voice, no matter what personal characteristics it may have, should be clear, audible and intelligible. These are requirements that anybody can fulfil, whether or not he or she has an attractive or less attractive voice. What are the features concerning the voice and elocution that commonly affect the presentation adversely? Monotony and gabbling must surely come high on the list.

Those who really wish to become as proficient as possible in the art of public speaking must make an opportunity to listen to their own voices. The pitch of the voice needs to be varied, sometimes reaching higher levels, sometimes lower, according to what is being said. It could be described as a dramatic effect.

Gabbled speech is an affliction which has become worse in recent and present times. Many TV presenters, who are supposed to be professional speakers, are gabblers. Thus 'I am going to' becomes 'I'm gonna'. When speaking in public we can usually speak more slowly than we do in normal conversation and increase effectiveness by doing so. On the theme of rate of speaking, many speakers fail to make sufficient use of the so-called pregnant pause – another oratorical trick in which both Churchill and Hitler excelled. The pause has two effects. It attracts attention, when the speaker stops for a while. It also allows an important point to sink in.

Eye-contact

What needs to be said about eye-contact applies only to presentations to smaller groups, i.e. when the speaker and audience are close enough to each other for eye-contact to be possible. Maintaining eye-contact is a technique which requires discipline. Speakers should remind themselves of the need to move their eyes from one extreme of the audience to the other. Most of us have probably experienced the discomfort caused by speakers who fix their gaze on one person in the audience and never move it throughout the length of the talk. Varying the eye-contact is a non-verbal message, which says 'I am talking to all of you'.

Sensitivity to the Audience

This subject, like eye-contact, also applies only to smaller audiences, where speakers and listeners can see each other's faces and expressions. Looking around the room, speakers will notice a variety of expressions throughout the talk. It would obviously be futile and a distraction from their main task, if speakers spent any time in trying to decipher all of these signs. However, they should be alert to messages that appear to be significant and general. For example, the room may be becoming stuffy and need ventilation. On a hot afternoon after lunch people may be more drowsy than normal, however interesting the presentation might be. Sensitive speakers will pick up these cues and give short breaks to allow the group members to refresh themselves. Puzzled looks on several faces will probably indicate that the speakers have not made a point sufficiently clear. They need to read the signs, ask if there is a problem and then clarify whatever has not been properly understood.

Humour

The judicious use of humour adds flavour to a talk like condiments to a meal. In after-dinner speaking, when the guests are probably in a relaxed mood, assisted by wine, it is permissible and desirable, perhaps, to have the audience 'rolling in the aisles'. Entertainment rather than edification is what is normally required on such occasions. When managers are talking to groups for more serious purposes, the comic-act would obviously be very much out of place. The importance of anecdotes has been mentioned, when the preparatory phase was being discussed. These may be humorous or they may not. Certainly speakers should not introduce humour gratuitously simply for purposes of amusement. A certain amount of humour can be helpful at the beginning to relax the speaker and the audience, but it must always be used in small doses. Used excessively, it can distract attention from the main message and may irritate some, if not all, members of the audience. What is needed is a readiness to use a quiet form of humour in an unforced, spontaneous way. The dour, deadpan delivery is not inspiring to the listeners. They want to hear a serious message, but they also would welcome a little light relief.

Spontaneous Speaking

Everything that has been said so far has concerned speaking based on preparation – the key to success. It does not happen, fortunately, too often that somebody is called upon to speak spontaneously, with little or no warning. These occasions tend to occur because the organizer of a function, such as a farewell party in the office, has forgotten to ask somebody 'to say a few words', or because the deputed speaker has failed to arrive for one reason or another. A few people who are able to speak at the drop of the proverbial hat, can switch on the speaking mechanism and words start to flow. Most of us would much prefer some warning, a chance to collect thoughts and to prepare in the systematic ways described in this chapter. The answer to the problem has been provided by Baden-Powell, the founder of the Scout movement, who chose 'Be prepared' as the movement's motto – a wise and inspired choice. Whenever people who hold some position of authority attend a meeting or function, where speeches will be made, they would be very well advised to ponder in advance what they would say, if called upon to speak at short notice. Since other speakers have already been appointed, it is obviously not necessary for them to spend much time preparing for a talk that they will fairly certainly not have to give. All that is needed are a few headings, arranged in an appropriate sequence, together with some suitable anecdotes. If the call comes, the deputy will be ready.

EXAMPLE OF PLAN FOR A TALK

Subject:	Prevention of heart disease
Speaker:	Company Medical Officer
Time:	30–40 minutes

A. INTRODUCTION
- Why is the subject important?
  - (1) Very high level of deaths and disability in the UK.
  - (2) Preventable by understanding causes and taking right action.
  - (3) In general too many people are indifferent.

B. MAIN CONTENTS
- What are main symptoms?   OHP 1
  - (1) Overweight, breathlessness, chest-pains
  - (2) High blood-pressure (not evident)
- What are main causes and remedies?
  - (1) Diet   OHP 2
  - (2) Exercise   OHP 3
  - (3) Alcohol consumption and smoking   OHP 4
  - (4) Stress   OHP 5
  - (5) Hereditary factors   OHP 6

C. CONCLUSIONS
- What are the main points to remember?
  - (1) Modern life-styles have considerably increased the risks
  - (2) It is preventable by:
    - (a) Awareness of main causative factors
    - (b) Personal discipline for healthy living

D. QUESTIONS

(3) CHAIRING MEETINGS AND DISCUSSIONS

Meetings and discussions are an essential part of working life. They may either be the formal kind of meeting, held in the company board room or the informal kind, held maybe at short notice in any convenient office. Discussions are a method commonly used in training courses by tutors for purposes of learning in groups. In all of these situations, a group of people gather to talk about a variety of subjects in order to achieve particular purposes. Like all other situations where people collaborate for specific reasons, there has to be a leader to make sure that the aim is clear, that there is a plan of action, that the plan is followed and to ensure that the group works as a team. Without leadership, discussions become a free-for-all. In a sense a meeting is a microcosm of the whole management process. Within the compass of meetings, many, if not all, of the phenomena that characterize working life may be seen. The same traits of individual and group behaviour need to be understood by group leaders to ensure effectiveness of meetings.

Meetings are held mainly for two reasons – to enable managers to pass on information to the members of their work-groups, or to discuss questions affecting work, for which answers have to be found. It may seem too obvious to require comment, but meetings must be necessary, and they must make a discernible contribution to the work of the group. Otherwise they can be notorious time-wasters. Whilst meetings which involve all the members of the group are being held, work stands still and productivity is halted for the duration of the meeting. If this happens, then there had better be good reasons for this interruption and worthwhile benefits. Meetings have a bearing on time-management. In some organizations managers seem to be obsessed with meetings. Attempts to contact them are regularly frustrated because, we are told, they are at a meeting. A device used by one manager, exasperated at the time he perceived to be wasted at meetings, was to arrange for his secretary to interrupt the meeting to say than an urgent matter had occurred, which required his immediate attention. Many of us no doubt have experienced similar feelings, especially when the meeting itself is inefficiently managed because the leader had not learned how to conduct meetings effectively.

As a very general rule, with all the reservations that this implies, it is the formal, scheduled, more ritualistic kinds of meetings that tend to be potential time-wasters. Good managers regularly hold informal meetings with the members of their group, whenever it is necessary to keep them informed or to give them a chance to share in making decisions that affect them. Bringing the group together for regular chats is also a very valuable way of developing team spirit.

Assuming that a meeting is necessary, we can now examine in detail what is needed to make it effective, i.e. achieving a necessary and worthwhile purpose. The broad requirements for effective practice will apply to all kinds of meetings and discussions. Successful meetings depend on leadership and group behaviour. They are a practical exemplification of the need for managers to have a basic knowledge of these subjects in order effectively to conduct meetings and discussions.

Preparation

As with all human activities, sound preparation is an essential foundation and requires the following action:

Preparing an agenda and arranging the items to be discussed in a logical order.

Planning the allocation of time. This is a very difficult task. One has only to think of parliamentary debates to realize that discussions of some topics could go on all night, if no time-limits are imposed. On the other hand, leaders should not stifle discussion which may well be necessary and important. They have a problem. They need to encourage a frank uninhibited exchange of views, but at the same time they cannot allow discussion to continue until it grinds to a halt through sheer exhaustion of the participants. The answer depends on the relative importance of topics and the leader's judgement. Any error should be made in the direction of allowing more time than may be necessary rather than less. It may well be that a whole morning or afternoon is needed, i.e. about three hours, to allow each topic to be adequately debated. If so, then it is important to build in a break of, say, fifteen to thirty minutes, so that the participants do not become stale and have a chance for refreshment and any other matters.

The leaders' judgement is also required to decide the order and the priorities of topics and approximately how much time should be allocated to each. They will need this guide when the meeting is under way to ensure that valuable time has not been slipping away unnoticed, when there are still several other important issues waiting to be discussed.

Deciding who needs to attend. This provision applies more to formal meetings, when the participants may come from anywhere within or outside the organization. When work-groups meetings are held, all its members would normally attend. The question of numbers attending really only affects the formal kinds of meetings. All the evidence of experience and research indicates problems when numbers are large. Obviously, one cannot put a definite figure on the right number of participants at a meeting: ideally, it is somewhere around five or six. In a meeting of this size it is much easier for participants to relate to one another. There is more time for each to speak. It is much easier for the leader to control. Control is the obvious problem when, say, fifteen to twenty people attend a meeting. There are probably more people who want to speak than there is time available. Forceful personalities can dominate, whilst the quieter ones are literally lost in the crowd. Because there are numerous people who may wish to speak, there are pressures of time. The answer is to keep the numbers as small as possible and to ensure that only people who really need to be present are requested to attend. In large organizations, there is a tendency for the person responsible for convening the meeting to invite people who might have only a minimal interest in the subject of the meeting. If others need only to be informed and are not really required to debate issues, then they can be sent a copy of the minutes.

Paying careful attention to the seating arrangement. Seating may seem at first to be a relatively minor detail. In fact, it has a very significant bearing on the success or failure of meetings. If people are to have meaningful, communicational relationships with each other during meetings they need to be situated in a way that will allow this to happen. They need eye-contact. This is where meetings with large numbers of people attending can be doomed to failure before they even start. At meetings of this kind it is quite common even nowadays for the members to be seated on either side of a long table with the chair at one end. With ten or more people sitting on either side of the table, it looks more like a banquet than a discussion. People at either end of the table cannot see one another and often cannot even hear what people at the other end of the table are saying. The discussion-leader has similar problems of communication. So why do they do it? Presumably because that is the way it has always been. The seating arrangement is determined by the length of the boardroom table. This kind of seating arrangement accentuates formality and inhibits the ebb and flow of debate that good meetings require. Films of cabinet meetings show that the tradition still persists at 10 Downing Street.

The obvious answer to the problem is to seat people in a circle. In this way the leader is included in the circle and everyone can see and hear everyone else. Moreover, the circle arrangement can accommodate quite large numbers of people – twenty or more. It should be used whatever the size of the meeting's membership.

Attending to environmental details. What has to be said about the environment is obvious and applies to any other similar work situation where concentration and attention are important. The main requirements are comfort, absence of distractions – e.g. telephones, external noise, interesting pictures, etc. – fresh air and refreshment.

Giving participants advance notice. Apart from the obvious details of time and place, it is necessary for people to know what is to be discussed and why. This applies to both formal and informal meetings. If important issues are to be discussed, then people must be given time to think about the subjects of the agenda before the meeting. They need to think of arguments for and against proposals, and of what they would advocate. They may also need time to look up relevant references or to do some preparatory reading. All of this is necessary and important, if proposals are to be scrutinized from all angles, before final decisions are taken.

Recording discussions and decisions. Arrangements need to be made in advance of meetings for somebody to be responsible for recording what was said and agreed. Usually this is done by the manager's secretary. Human memory is notoriously unreliable. People will stoutly deny that they said what was attributed to them, or may maintain that they said something which others cannot recall. In any case, managers cannot be sure when at some future date they may wish to refer to discussions and decisions taken at sometime in the past, possibly by their predecessors in the job. Recording the essence of meetings is, of course, standard practice for formal meetings. The same procedure is also necessary for the informal meetings that managers regularly hold.

During Discussion

(a) **Leaders' tasks**. They should:

1. Begin by ensuring that the purpose of the meeting and agenda items are fully understood.
2. See that the discussions follow a logical order and keep to the point. People in discussion do not naturally discipline themselves. They can very easily wander away from the main highway of the discussion. This often happens when participants indulge in what the textbooks call special pleading, i.e. they have an axe to grind and persist in pursuing themes of particular interest and concern only to themselves.
3. Manage the time as planned in the preparation phase. It is one thing to make plans for the allocation of time to topics, and another to see that the timetable is followed in practice. This does not mean that leaders have to be excessively punctilious, but they must not allow valuable time to be wasted on subjects of minor importance, when some issues need all the time they can get.
4. See that all questions are thoroughly explored. There are always alternative options to proposals for action. One of these is to leave things as they are. If there is a strong consensus for a particular

proposal, it is particularly important to be on guard against the 'group think' phenomenon, described earlier during the discussions of group behaviour. Minorities – even of one – need to be very carefully heeded. They could save the group from a bad decision.

5. Ensure that everyone has a fair chance to contribute. This means keeping in check stronger personalities, who would otherwise dominate the discussion, and encouraging the quieter members to say what they want. Silence at meetings by no means indicates that people have nothing important or worthwhile to say. It might do so. On the other hand, it sometimes indicates diffidence. This can only be overcome by encouragement from the discussion leader.

6. Focus attention on *what* is right, rather than *who* is right. Being an interpersonal activity, meetings tend to focus attention on personalities. It matters not who makes the most worthwhile contributions. The meeting is not a competition to see who can come up with the best answers. It is a team effort. All that matters is that collectively they reach sound conclusions. This is one of the important functions of leadership.

7. Meanings are checked and misunderstandings clarified. Discussion leaders have to be very alert to listen and concentrate intently on what people are saying. If anything is said that they feel might be misinterpreted, they must check, asking, for example: 'What do you mean by . . . ?' or 'Have I understood you correctly. When you say – do you mean –?'

8. Deal firmly with any signs of negative conflict or negative emotional behaviour. Leaders are concerned all the time, whether conducting meetings or pursuing the objectives of work, to see that members of the team collaborate and direct their efforts constructively towards positive purposes. R. F. Bales, a psychologist who made a special study of group behaviour, noted that apart from those who were concerned with task and team needs, there were some whose behaviour he described as negative emotional. Since it takes all sorts to make a world, there is always the possibility that some immature people may use meetings to exhibit their psychological hang-ups. They are more concerned with self than advancing the progress of the group.

9. Summarize discussions. At the end of a discussion on each particular topic, leaders should summarize the main points and agreements that have been made. This will confirm the progress that the group has made and at the same time it should allow the group-members to

make any amendments, if they wish. To enable this to happen, leaders should ask the group whether the summary is a fair and accurate account and whether they wish to add or subtract anything.

(b) Leaders' demeanour

When conducting meetings and discussions, group leaders need to use the same democratic-participative style that is effective for most situations in the normal course of daily work. Therefore, they should:

1. Exercise a quiet, but firm control.
2. Aim to create a calm, relaxed, good-humoured atmosphere. Group members are more likely to feel comfortable and willing to say what they truly feel if the climate of the meeting is not threatening, not too sombre and not without a laugh or two, or at least a smile. In the same vein, it is the leaders' task to see that things are kept in perspective and discussions do not become overheated.
3. Avoid imposing their views on the group. They should ask relevant questions, listen to what people are saying and be psychologically alert in picking up any cues, e.g. non-verbal signs, that may be significant. Members of the Cabinet during World War 2 were heard to complain that a meeting with Winston Churchill in the chair was a monologue. Whether this is true or not, the problem with the authoritarian style of chairing meetings is the same as that in the work situation. Group-members' views which may be very important to the decision-making process do not get a chance to be aired. They give in with resignation, recognizing that the views of the boss will prevail, whatever they may say. Any sycophants in the group can be relied upon not to say what they themselves truly believe, but to agree with what the boss says or to say what they think he or she wants to hear. Democratic-participative leaders do not relinquish their authority by following this style. When all members of the group have had their say, they give their views and decide which proposals carry most weight.

After Discussion

When the discussion has ended, group leaders should summarize what has been said and agreed in the whole discussion and ask if anyone wishes to make any amendments. On the basis of notes made during the meeting, this summary should then be recorded in writing. Copies should then be passed to those who took part in the discussion for any further comment and amendment and for retention. The manager who has led the meeting will keep a copy for future reference.

So far, we have been concerned mainly with the practical measures that are necessary to make the best use of meetings. This is a question of organization and planning and is obviously very important. At the same time, the effectiveness of meetings depends very much on the psychological insight of managers in the chair. Meetings are like a pond. There is much more happening beneath the surface than meets the eye. In addition to the apparent task of discussing the various items of the agenda, agreeing and deciding on action, all kinds of other personal and interpersonal behaviour are probably going on at the same time which are by no means obvious. Some individuals may have a hidden agenda – motives or objectives of their own outside the scope of the official agenda of the meeting, e.g. to impress the manager or colleagues, to dominate, to air personal feelings, etc.

The balloons that we sometimes see attached to people's heads in comic strips, marked 'thinks', are probably also present during meetings. 'Thinks' might include such silent thoughts, for example, as 'I wish he would get to the point'. 'Here we go again. Smith on his usual hobby horse'. 'When is the manager ever going to learn how to run a meeting?' People at meetings may say that they agree with something, when in truth they have doubts, or they may remain silent in disagreement.

Discussions and natterings that sometimes occur after meetings are facets of this covert behaviour and at the same time symptoms of the deficiencies of the meeting itself. People sometimes get together in small groups and voice views and feelings that should have emerged at the meeting.

Managers need to be aware that meetings are seldom, if ever, concerned solely with the task in hand. They cannot be expected to know what may be going on beneath the surface. However, if they know the characteristics of the individual members of their groups and have established open discussion as a norm, it is less likely that members of the group will be inclined to whinge after the meeting about the way it was conducted or about decisions.

EXERCISE ON ASKING AND LISTENING

- The exercise requires three people who take turns to act as interviewer, interviewee and observer.
- Each interview lasts for ten minutes.
- The subject of the interview is the interviewee's present or a previous job, as preferred.

Interviewer's Task

- Question the interviewee about the job, concentrating on asking as many questions as possible that begin with HOW, WHY, WHERE, WHAT, WHEN, WHO.
- Stop and rephrase a badly framed question, if you wish.
- In addition to the bare facts, try to ask about the interviewee's feelings, problems, motives, attitudes, reasons, etc.
- Completing the survey of the job in the time allowed is not important. The emphasis is on question-technique.
- When the interview is over, the next phase is to test listening.
- Give the interviewee a summary of what he/she has told you, including feelings, problems, motives, attitudes, etc. (This is an especially important indication of good listening.)

Interviewee's Task

- Give a truthful and honest account of yourself.
- Avoid helping the interviewer. If he or she asks a question that could be answered by 'yes' or 'no', simply say 'yes' or 'no'. Do not volunteer information.
- Listen carefully to the interviewer's summary after the interview and comment on how accurate this is and how carefully the interviewer listened to what you said.

Observer's Task

- Take a sheet of paper and make two columns: (1) Open questions; (2) Yes/No questions.
- Put a tick in the appropriate column for each question the interviewer asks.
- Keep an eye on the clock and stop the interview after ten minutes.

- After the interview and the interviewer's summary and interviewee's remarks, report to the interviewer on questioning technique. How many questions were open? How many were in the Yes/No column?

EXERCISE ON SPEAKING TO GROUPS

- Prepare a talk on Health and Safety at Work (see Chapter 10(1)) to be given to your work-group to last for approximately twenty to thirty minutes (see example at the end of this chapter.
- In preparing the talk try to include actual examples to illustrate the talk.
- If practicable, give the talk to your work-group, having first rehearsed it either by yourself of with a friend or colleague.
- Ask a colleague to make an assessment of its effectiveness.

CHAPTER 4

Making Sound Judgements

BASIC QUESTIONS
1 **What part does judgement play when managers are carrying out the personnel functions of management?**
2 **What are the problems of judgement and their causes?**
3 **How might these problems be mitigated in practice?**

Judgement dominates managers' work. It needs, therefore, special consideration in any book on the subject of management. Because of their leading role, managers are required to make judgements of varying kinds almost every day of their working lives. Some concern trivial matters; others are crucially important for the achievement of group and organizational aims and objectives. In their role as leaders of people, managers have to answer questions of the following kinds:

- How is effective performance to be defined and assessed?
- Which candidates for employment are likely to be able to meet the requirements for effective performance?
- Are employees performing their work as required, and if not what action is needed?
- What effect have developmental and training activities had on actual subsequent work-performance?
- Are any employees falling below required standards in terms of efficiency or discipline, and if so what action needs to be taken?

If managers produce the wrong answers to these and other similar questions, the consequences could obviously be very serious. So whilst it is extremely important to find the right answers, the judgements on which the answers depend are always human and, therefore, inherently subjective and fallible.

Standards of judgements inevitably fluctuate and are inconsistent within one judge over a period of time and between any two judges. Ask somebody to assess an essay now and again in five years' time. In all probability the assessments will vary with the passage of time. Ask several people to mark the same essay and there could well be significant differences between the highest and lowest ratings. What one sees as a virtue, another sees as a sin. We see examples of the problem every day. Judges at ice-skating contests hold up their mark-cards and show surprising differences of views about the same performance. Margaret Thatcher's performance as Prime Minister produced a significant, judgemental controversy. Some regarded her as a great leader who was resolute, inspiring and successful in restoring national pride and economic progress. Others took a quite different view. They saw her as a jingoistic, materialistic, autocrat, mainly responsible for the widening gap between rich and poor.

Some people are exceptionally confident of their abilities to judge others accurately after only a brief acquaintance, claiming at the same time that they are seldom wrong. Some senior managers are prone to believe that they must be better judges than their juniors because of longer and wider experience. All the research on the subject shows that these assumptions are not justified.

It has been said that one characteristic distinguishing psychologists from others is that psychologists are much less confident of their ability to judge other people accurately. Examples abound to show how wrong we can often be when judging people. Confidence tricksters depend on this human weakness for their livelihood. It is not only gullible old ladies swindled out of their savings by smooth-tongued crooks who are taken in. All kinds of people are regularly deceived and make bad judgements, because they approach the task in an instinctive, emotional, unsystematic way. What is to be said about the kind of judgement by an appointments board that allows a bogus doctor to take up a medical appointment and to practise for some time before being unmasked?

Consider the following example, based on the appraisal of work-performance. Manager A assesses Employee X as tactless. He feels threatened by any members of his staff who appear to be too forceful in speaking their minds. Manager B, on the other hand, sees X's behaviour as a virtue. He likes people to say what they truly think so long as they are not gratuitously offensive. Accordingly, he describes X as somebody who can be relied upon to give frank and honest opinions. He marks X favourably. So here we have the same behaviour being rated as a minus point by one manager and as a plus point by another.

These kind of differences are occurring all the time in the world of work. In all of the examples, quoted above, the behaviour of those being assessed is the constant factor. The variables are the ratings of the judges. So why do people judge the same behaviour quite differently? The roots of the problem lie in the individual differences, already discussed, and the effects of these differences on perceptions and judgements. Furthermore, human beings are emotional creatures. They are ever prone to make illogical, capricious, gut-reaction judgements. As the nursery jingle puts it: 'I do not like thee Dr Fell, the reason why I cannot tell, but this I know and know full well, I do not like thee Dr Fell'.

The effects of individual differences on judgement can be seen in the following example, this time based on an employee-selection. Candidate X is being considered for a managerial post. She is suitable in all respects in terms of qualifications and experience. All the reports of confidential referees are favourable. Here are some of her background details. She is a woman in her late thirties. She was educated at an inner city comprehensive school and then at a polytechnic where she gained a first-class honours degree in sociology. She is a pacifist, an atheist and an active member of the Anti-Blood Sports League.

One of the selectors is a male, aged sixty-five. Educated at a well-known, public school and Cambridge University, he has a degree in science. He is a retired Army Colonel, a devout Christian, Chairman of the Church Council, Chairman of the local Conservative Party, a Justice of the Peace and Master of Foxhounds. Hunting is his favourite leisure activity. This is, of course, a hypothetical fantasy, but it well illustrates the possible effects of individual differences on the process of judgement. Despite candidate X's suitability for the post, how far, might we ask, could the extreme differences in the backgrounds of a selector and candidate affect the selector's judgement?

Since so much depends on managers' judgements, what is to be done? The first step is to be aware of the existence of the problem and the effects of individual differences on judgements. The next step is to mitigate its worst effects as far as possible by being systematic in approaching all situations requiring judgement. A systematic approach to judgement has the following stages:

1. Definition of the required behaviour and performance, preferably by discussion and agreement. These are the criteria.
2. Observation and assessment of actual behaviour, noting examples. This is the evidence.
3. Comparison of the evidence with the criteria to form judgements as a basis for action.
4. Analysis of the range of possible options and choice of whatever seems best to meet the requirements of the criteria.

The inevitable subjectivity of the process of judgement can be further mitigated by involving others. Peter Drucker's comment on the importance of a variety of opinions in the process of decision-making is pertinent. Proposals for decisions that have important consequences need to be tested to see whether they can survive a close scrutiny and rigorous examination unscathed, or whether they need to be revised or even abandoned altogether. This has implications for management styles. The autocrat operating in solitary isolation is likely to make unsound judgements because they are not tested or contested by other people. It explains why dictatorial regimes regularly end in catastrophe. Democratic-participative managers invite members of their teams to have their say and are likely, therefore, to avoid the mistakes of the autocrat.

The benefits of inviting other opinions in the process of making judgements and decisions can be clearly seen in two very important personnel functions, namely employee-selection and performance-appraisal. In assessing the potential of candidates for employment each member of a selection board should be required to justify his or her judgements to the other members of the board. If, for example, a board member considers that a candidate does not meet one of the specified requirements, he or she should be challenged to produce valid evidence to support the judgement. In performance appraisal, which, as we shall see, should be based on a two-way discussion, either the manager or the person being appraised should ask the other to produce evidence to support views, especially if these seem to be unsound.

Judgement cannot be taught, but managers can be helped in training courses on management to become more aware of the importance of making judgements as sound as they can possibly be, of the inherent problems and how they might be mitigated by a systematic approach.

Here are two examples of training exercises which experience has shown to be very useful in helping managers to deal effectively with the judgement process. When simulating selection interviews, mock candidates are sometimes used who have already successfully passed the real selection process and are already working for the employing organization. This information is withheld from the trainee-selectors. If a mock candidate is rejected by the trainee selection-board, as they sometimes are, there is food for thought about the judgement process. Who was right? Was it the real selection-board, or was it the trainee-board? How are the differing judgements to be explained?

The second exercise is based on performance-appraisal. Trainee managers are required to define criteria for effective performance for one of the jobs in their work-groups. They are then told to think of one particular job-holder and to appraise his or her performance of the job, based on the criteria and actual evidence of performance. The final stage of the exercise is to subject the criteria and the evidence produced by each trainee to a rigorous examination by their colleagues. It regularly happens that evidence, on which judgements are based, is found to be of doubtful validity.

The criteria-evidence-judgement system can never provide a complete answer to the abiding problems of human judgement. Nevertheless, it is the only means whereby what would otherwise be a totally fortuitous process can become something more cool, calculated, effective and fair.

EXERCISE ON MAKING SOUND JUDGEMENTS

- Think of at least three examples of unsound judgements that you believe yourself, relatives or acquaintances have made.
- Examine these judgements critically in the light of the criteria-evidence-judgement system described in this chapter.
- What would you say were the causes of the unsound judgements?
- With hindsight, how might these unsound judgements have been avoided or mitigated in their effects?

CHAPTER 5

Defining Requirements for Effective Performance – Job Analysis

BASIC QUESTIONS

1 Why could defining the requirements for the effective performance of work be aptly described as fundamentally important?
2 What items does a detailed analysis of a job include?
3 What kind of criteria might be used for assessing the corporate
   effectiveness of a group or organization?

The effective performance of individuals, groups and organizations is a
primary concern for managers at all levels. When all is said and done,
producing required results is their *raison d'être*. Defining the requirements
for effective performance is crucially important to the systematic and
effective management of people at work. The definition provides the
criteria in the judgement process and has two purposes. First, it prescribes
what is required for the purposes of jobs to be achieved. Secondly, it
provides the datum-line with reference to which the achievement of the
defined requirements are to be assessed. The definition is equally important to job-holders. They need to know where they stand, what they are
required to do and achieve. As we shall see later, providing this information is an important part of the induction process. One of the first tasks
that managers must carry out when meeting newly appointed staff, is to

ensure that they fully understand what they are expected to do. In broad terms, the effective performance of work includes the following requirements:

1. Professional, vocational competence.
2. Harmonious, collaborative relationships with work-colleagues, with the employing organization and its clients.
3. Positive attitudes towards work.
4. Ability to develop competence in work-performance.

The effective performance of work demands much more than the ability to meet the requirements of the component tasks in technical terms. How, for example, are we to rate the effectiveness of the employee who is the most proficient member of a work-group in terms of technical ability, but at the same time finds it difficult to collaborate with others and regularly upsets colleagues and clients?

In defining the requirements for the effective performance of work we need two lists – one to describe the job itself, the job description, and the other to describe the personal characteristics needed to fulfil the requirements of the job description, the person specification.

Because of the basic importance of these criteria to the effective management of people at work, the task of job analysis to produce these definitions needs to be carried out thoroughly, comprehensively and accurately. It may be carried out by an organization's own personnel specialists, by external consultants or by local-line managers. A variety of methods may be used, such as direct observation and recording of job-holders at work, interviews with job-holders and their managers, diaries kept by job-holders to record activities and incidents, or by questionnaires. These methods are invariably time-consuming and costly. Specialist-analysts are most likely to be employed where the required results justify the time and costs. They might be used, for example, in large organizations where a number of people perform the same categories of work. In this way job analysis would ensure that definitions of jobs are comprehensive, accurate and standardized throughout the whole organization, and cost-effective in ensuring that only necessary requirements are included.

There is another important consideration that affects possible costs of job analysis carried out by specialists. The requirements for the effective performance of work do not stand still. They change with changing times. This is especially true in the present times of rapid change. Job descriptions and person specifications need, therefore, to be regularly revised.

Quite often the task of job analysis for the members of the work-group is the responsibility of local line-managers. It is important that they fully understand the key importance of this task in their role as managers of people. It is not a task to be carried out by managers alone. They need to discuss the criteria with the job-holders themselves who, after some experience, are in a unique position to say what their jobs require. As we shall see later, when discussing performance-appraisal, a discussion of possible changes that might be needed in the specified job requirements is the first item on the agenda. If these requirements need to be changed, this obviously affects the assessment of performance.

The Job Description

The items to be included in the job description obviously depend on the requirements of specific jobs. Those which are common to all jobs are:

- Job title.
- Purpose of the job, its relationship to the function of the work-group and the employing organization.
- Managerial post to which the job-holder is responsible.
- Staff and resources for whom and for which the job-holder is responsible.
- Main component tasks of the job, which together must be effectively performed to achieve the purpose of the job.
- Conditions and terms of employment.

Person Specification

The person specification describes the kind of person needed to perform the job effectively. It will be needed in particular for assessing the suitability of job applicants and for assessing the performance of existing employees and their needs. If all of these requirements are systematically analysed, it can be seen that they fall under one of three interdependent categories, i.e. knowledge, skills, attitudes and personal attributes. For example, effective doctors need to have a comprehensive and detailed knowledge of the physical and mental characteristics of the human species, male and female, of possible diseases and their causes, of available and appropriate remedies. They need to have skills in the diagnosis and treatment of ailments. Some, such as surgeons, need specialist skills.

They all need interpersonal skills in order to deal with a wide range of people with whom they have to relate – patients, other specialists, nurses, administrators, etc. The importance of attitudes and personal attributes has already been mentioned. What do doctors require in this category of requirements to be effective? For the medical profession it might be proposed that the following attitudes and attributes are important: caring, sensitive, thorough, conscientious, co-operative, tolerant, patient, in control of emotions, open-minded and flexible in outlook. The list of necessary requirements could seem endless and universally applicable. When completed it might seem that only a paragon could qualify for employment. All the same, attitudes and personal attributes are such important factors in determining success or failure in jobs that they need to be very carefully considered and defined. It is necessary to identify those which are especially important to the job in question.

In addition to the definition of the person specification in terms of the categories described above, it is also necessary to describe requirements in terms of qualifications and experience. Depending on particular organizational requirements, the person specification may include other headings, such as age, appearance, health, special conditions (e.g. travel, unsocial hours, weekend work, etc.). Special care is needed in the preparation of person specifications to ensure that the requirements they include truly and accurately match the needs of the job. There is a tendency sometimes to specify qualifications and experience that the job does not, in fact, need. Certain overseas employers are notorious in specifying doctorates as essential qualifications for all appointments for university teaching staff.

Nowadays people who produce person specifications need to be especially careful because of the requirements of employment law. The enactments concerned with unfair practice in discriminating against job applicants on grounds of sex, race or disability have a bearing on person specifications. Prospective employees can no longer be excluded from consideration for employment on these grounds. The only acceptable exceptions apply to jobs where the nature of the work must obviously be filled by a man or a woman. It would be perfectly legal, therefore, to specify that a male actor is required to play the part of Hamlet, or that a woman is needed to work as an attendant in the women's toilet. An example of a Job Description and Person Specification is given at the end of the chapter.

Most managers are mainly concerned with the requirements for the effective performance of individual employees. Ultimately, however, it is the performance of groups and organizations as a whole that matter. The effective performances of individuals collectively contribute to the achievement of these goals. The criteria for success in the total terms will vary depending on the nature and purposes of each organization. They are often not too easy to measure, but that is no reason for avoiding the task. How can any organization achieve effectiveness, if it has no criteria for measuring achievement? The kinds of criteria that might be produced to assess total effectiveness are, for example:

- productivity levels
- profit levels
- customer satisfaction
- levels of complaints
- accident rates
- levels of mistakes at work
- job-satisfaction of employees
- rates of absence and sickness
- levels of labour turnover
- effects of training on performance

JOB DESCRIPTION AND PERSON SPECIFICATION FOR STAFF TRAINERS

Job title
Staff Trainer at the Training Centre, Caledonian Engineering Company, Glasgow.

Purpose
To provide training courses for supervisors and junior managers in management and related subjects that cost-effectively meet their job needs.

Responsible to
Director of the Training Centre.

Responsible for
- Course support staff allocated to courses
- Funds and material resources allocated for courses

Main tasks essential for effective performance

1. Design and provision of cost-effective training courses to meet the needs of managers and staffs, based on close liaison with managers in order to:
   (a) identify training needs;
   (b) design and provide needs-related training;
   (c) assess cost-effectiveness of training;
   (d) amend and improve training as necessary.

2. Selection and appointment of part-time tutors/speakers capable of effective performance of training tasks.
3. Monitoring performance of part-time tutors/speakers and remedying any deficiencies.
4. Effectively managing the support staff in terms of work-performance and welfare.
5. Managing the allocated finances and material resources as cost-effectively as possible.
6. Contributing to courses as course leader and tutor/speaker.

Person Specification (1)

THE REQUISITE KNOWLEDGE, SKILLS, ATTITUDES AND PERSONAL ATTRIBUTES

Knowledge

Notes

- Purpose of the employing organization and its component divisions

  The job-holder must be completely conversant with the work of the organization in order to meet its training needs.

- Requirements for the design and provision of cost-effective training

  The job-holder will be given basic initial and subsequent updating and developmental training courses.

Skills

Interpersonal/communicational

These are crucial to effective performance. The job-holder relates to a wide range of employees. He/she must be very skilful as a speaker/tutor.

Managerial and leadership	The job-holder needs effectively to manage the training and material resources, to manage the training function, and to be an effective leader of staff and trainees.

Key attitudes and attributes

● Commitment and enthusiasm	Job-holder must have strong belief in the value of training. Trainer-effectiveness depends much on hard work and attention to detail.
● Reliability	Job-holder must be somebody trusted to do his/her best at all times.
● Flexibility and adaptability	Job-holder must be a constant learner, ever ready to meet changing circumstances and to improve own knowledge and skills.
● Tolerance and patience	These qualities are especially important since the job requires continual relationships with a wide variety of people.
● Imagination	Job-holder must always be seeking better ways to train people.

Person Specification (2)

SPECIFIC REQUIREMENTS AND QUALIFICATIONS

Appearance	**Notes**
Smart and tidy	This is more important than it may seem. A number of managers and trainees judge by appearances and are put off by slovenliness.

Age	
30–50 (approximately)	This is not crucial, but anyone under 30 years of age is unlikely to have acquired sufficient experience and credibility to perform the job effectively.

Health

Very good

There should be no history of bad health likely to recur. The job is physically and mentally demanding. Frequent absences for health reasons would cause serious problems in finding a suitable replacement, especially at short notice.

Qualifications

GCE A Level standard. Higher qualifications and any qualifications relevant to training are a bonus.

Because of the instructional nature of the job a sound educational background is essential.

Experience

A proven sound record as a manager (probably at least five years). Any experience in training work would be a bonus

To instruct others effectively and credibly, the job-holder must have had a successful managerial career him/herself. Previous training experience is desirable but not essential, as basic training for the job will be provided.

Special conditions

The job-holder must be prepared to work sometimes in the evenings

Because training at the centre is residential, training regularly takes place in the evenings.

EXERCISE ON DEFINING REQUIREMENTS FOR EFFECTIVE PERFORMANCE

- Refer to the examples of a job description and person specification (74–77).
- Define the requirements of your own job and the members of your work-group in the same format and similar language.

CHAPTER 6

Selecting the Right People for Employment

BASIC QUESTIONS

1 Why is selecting the right people a crucial judgemental task for managers?
2 What are the basic problems of employee-selection?
3 What are the sources of evidence available to employee-selectors?
4 What are the limitations of the interview as a selection method?
5 How may the interview be used to best effect?

The achievement of group and organizational goals depends very much on the collective performance of individual employees. The initial selection of these employees is, therefore, the most important of the judgements that managers have to make. The consequences of mistakes in these appointments may be far-reaching and very costly. Incompetent performers may cause a variety of problems – low levels of performance and productivity, costly and serious mistakes, avoidable accidents, increased labour turnover, increased training needs and costs, problems in relationships with colleagues and clients, etc. Employers need, therefore, to realize just how fundamentally important the selection task is, and to devote to it the attention and resources it requires. Whilst employee-selection is a fundamentally important task, at the same time it involves making predictions about how people are likely to behave in future situations. On the basis of human, fallible judgement, selectors are required to predict whether people, who more often than not are complete strangers, are likely to meet the criteria for effective performance of jobs – and this on very brief acquaintance in stressful circumstances.

In broad, general terms the selection-prediction is concerned with the following areas of potential competence:

1. **Vocational, professional** – the ability to perform effectively the tasks of the jobs.
2. **Interpersonal** – the ability to relate co-operatively and harmoniously with work colleagues and clients.
3. **Organizational** – the ability to adapt to the culture of the employing organization and to fit successfully into its ways.
4. **Developmental** – the capacity to learn, to develop abilities, to improve performance, to accept increased responsibilities and to become of increasing value to the employer.

The problems of predicting the potential to meet these kinds of criteria are inescapable and can never be eliminated. However, they can and must be mitigated by the following methodical approach to the task.

Awareness of the nature and problems of employee selection
Manager-selectors need to undertake the task with full knowledge of the limitations and difficulties of forecasting behaviour. The task should be approached with humility and certainly not the over-confidence to judge other people that is usually the result of ignorance of the problems.
Use of the 'criteria-evidence-judgement' system
It involves defining very carefully and accurately the criteria for effective performance by means of job analysis, acquiring the best possible evidence of candidates' potential, and comparing the evidence with the criteria as the basis of a systematic judgement.
Regularly monitoring the selection system
Once people have passed through the selection process and have worked for some time in their jobs, the accuracy of the selection predictions can be assessed. It is the proof of the pudding. This is why some employees do not finally confirm appointments until the completion of a probationary period of say, six to twelve months. They regard the selection decision as tentative and confirm or cancel appointments on the evidence of actual work-performance.

Although the probationary system could be considered as causing some uncertainty, it is undoubtedly an effective means of meeting the problems of prediction. The efficacy of the selection process should be checked by the personnel department by collecting information from managers about the actual performance of recently appointed employees. In this way, employing organizations can assess how effective their selection systems are, whether too many unsuitable people are slipping through the net, and what remedial actions may be needed to improve the situation. At the same time, managers should use their own initiative in reporting any instances where recently selected employees are clearly not able to meet the requirements of the job.

Training managers for employee-selection tasks

This is an essential requirement in order to make the best possible use of a limited method. The considerable research that has taken place into the subject of employee-selection over many years has produced the following conclusions:

(a) Because of the inherent problems of predicting human behaviour in future unknown situations, the selection process will always have a limited level of achievable efficiency. This level can be optimized if selectors are properly trained for the task. Training should cover: the nature and problems of employee-selection; the implications of employment law; a systematic approach to the task, based on a criteria-evidence-judgement system; practice in conducting interviews which simulate reality as closely as possible, including the use of CCTV, so that trainee-selectors may learn from recordings of their own performance. A manager who has to undertake any form of employee-selection should apply for a training course, if the employing organization does not arrange for training.

(b) When selectors have received no training along these lines and are, therefore, unaware of the basic problems, nor of ways whereby they may be mitigated, the selection process becomes little more than a lottery.

THE ESSENTIALS OF AN EFFECTIVE SYSTEM

STAGE I Defining the Criteria for Effective Performance

These criteria are described in the Job Description and Person Specification obtained by Job Analysis. The definition of the criteria for effective performance is an absolute essential for systematic and, therefore, effective employee-selection. Without it the process becomes meaningless. It needs to be emphasized that employee-selectors are not normally looking for fully effective performers at this stage. Their task is to judge whether candidates appear to have the potential to meet the criteria for effective performance after a period of work experience and training.

STAGE 2   Collecting as much Reliable and Valid Evidence as Possible

Before the possible sources of evidence are considered, the concepts of reliability and validity need to be discussed in their psychological context and in terms of their significance to the process of assessing suitability for employment.

Reliability and Validity

The reliability of a selection method is concerned with consistency. A method is described as reliable if it produces similar results when the assessment or measurement is repeated. Reliability means that the measuring agent is constant. The variables are the subjects being measured or assessed. For example, a ruler could be described as a reliable agent for measuring anything, wood or cheese in summer or winter in any part of the world. Validity means that the method truly measures or assesses what it purports to do. For example, how valid a test of managerial capabilities is the following question, put to candidates during a selection interview?

'What are the essential requirements for managerial effectiveness?'

The question is valid only in so far as it may tell interviewers whether candidates know what the requirements are. It has the same validity as an examination question. The answer would reveal little or nothing that was valid about their potential to be effective managers in practice. They might well be able to give perfect textbook answers, and yet be amongst the most incompetent managers that ever drew breath, when it comes to performing the manager's job.

It needs to be said at the outset that absence of evidence must not be taken as an indication that candidates are deficient in particular requirements of a job. If, for example, physical courage were an important requirement for a job, some candidates might well be able to meet this criterion, if appointed. At the same time, it could well be that there has been no opportunity in their lives to date to enable this quality to be demonstrated, and that there is no reliable or valid test in the selection process, designed to enable physical courage to be revealed and assessed.

There are three main sources of evidence available to employee-selectors – written information, the interview and a range of tests. These will now be examined in turn with particular emphasis on the interview. The interview requires special attention because it is common to every selection process, is often the only method used, and requires considerable knowledge and skill for effective use.

Written Information

Written information includes the application documents and reports by referees either as confidential references or as testimonials. Information of this kind is used as a basis for choosing candidates to undergo the selection process from the total number of applicants. In view of what has already been said about the subjectivity and fallibility of human judgement, this sift needs to be approached with considerable care. The selection process, by its very nature, is discriminatory. It is important, therefore, that it should be as fair as possible. The information available to employee-selectors at the sift stage is, after all, only on paper. It has not been subjected to the probing inquiry of an interview to amplify or clarify statements made. For example, an applicant once included mountaineering as an interest on his application form. Questioned about this at interview he revealed that the interest was academic, i.e. studying the literature of the subject.

Studying the application documents with great care and avoiding unwarranted assumptions, employee-selectors need to produce three categories – applicants who are apparently suitable, apparently unsuitable and marginal. Attention should then be directed to the marginal applicants. Their claims require a further scrutiny to make a final decision as to whether they should be accepted or rejected. Of course, if the number of apparently suitable applicants is considered sufficient as it is, then the employee-selectors may well decide that there is no need to select additional candidates from the marginal group.

In addition to the information supplied by applicants themselves, other evidence may be given by people qualified to pass judgement on applicants' suitability. The value of this information is obviously liable to considerable variation. Testimonials which are open reports acquired by the applicants are not usually rated very highly in popular esteem. Since applicants have chosen their own authors of testimonials and will see what has been written about them, it is most unlikely that anything other than favourable comments will be made. Despite these reservations, testimonials are not necessarily completely valueless to employee-selectors. They can be useful in confirming the factual evidence of an applicant's career and achievements. Furthermore, if several writers of testimonials for the same person all comment favourably on the same characteristics, this could be regarded as useful evidence. The writers will have expressed their opinions independently without collusion and reached the same conclusions.

Confidential reports are not normally required until applicants have been selected as candidates for the selection process. Although candidates usually have some choice in nominating referees, it is also normal for employers to specify what kind of people these should be, e.g. former employers, principals of colleges, etc. When asking referees to provide confidential reports on applicants, it is important that employers should inform the referees of their selection criteria. In this way, referees are better able to comment on the kind of information that employers wish to have. There is an important caveat that needs to be made about referees' confidential reports. Valuable though they may sometimes be, they should never be regarded as gospel truth, simply because the authors once held a position of authority over candidates. These people are just as capable of unfair or perhaps even spiteful comment as any other human beings. If the relationship between the candidate and the referee was bad, why should any denigration of candidates be accepted automatically as valid, especially when they have no opportunity to read what has been said about them in confidence, nor to comment on or contest statements.

Finally, disgraceful though it may be, it is not entirely unknown for employers to give glowing, confidential reports for candidates in the hope that this may enable them to rid themselves of employees whom for some reason they would sooner be without.

The Selection Interview

Whatever other method employers may use, the interview is essential for the following reasons: to meet candidates face-to-face; to examine credentials and to investigate written information in depth; to obtain any additional information required; to give candidates a chance to ask any questions they may wish to raise. Whilst the interview is an essential part of the selection process and is often the only method used, it has very serious limitations in terms of reliability and validity. What are these limitations?

1. Unless candidates are already employees of the organization or are known in some other way, the interview is usually a fairly brief meeting between strangers in an unnatural, stressful situation. We are all well aware of how we may change our initial views of people after longer and closer acquaintance. The interview puts the selectors in a situation where, inevitably, they form subjective first impressions. Anyone with experience of assessment centres, where candidates are subjected to a variety of tests over a number of days, will readily confirm that first impressions formed at interviews regularly need to be revised. Some people are seen in a more favourable light than initially; others are seen in a less favourable light. Had the selection decisions rested entirely on opinions formed at interviews, then these candidates would have been inaccurately assessed.

2. Because of the unnatural nature of the selection interview, the behaviour of candidates in this situation should be regarded with very considerable caution. We all inevitably make some kinds of judgements about people on first acquaintance. It is very difficult for interviewers to discipline themselves to avoid making hasty judgements. The way that people behave at interviews tells us little or nothing about how they might behave in the course of their daily lives and work, and yet selection interviewers regularly attach far too much importance to interview-behaviour when forming judgements of suitability for employment. A major organization once issued its employee-selectors with a form for assessing candidates at interview. The items listed were: appearance; powers of expression; mental alertness; reasoning powers; independence of thought; initiative; range and depth of interests. There must surely have been all kinds of other criteria that effective performance of the job required. Most of the items in this list are much more concerned with candidates' performance and demeanour during the thirty to forty minutes of the interview itself.

3. Human beings are not reliable measuring agents. In the judgmental situation of the selection interview, they will vary in the following ways:
   (a) People react instinctively to others. Sexual attraction is a good example of this. Interviewers will tend to like some candidates and dislike others. Interviewer-colleagues may have opposite likes and

dislikes. These feelings cannot be explained rationally. Nevertheless, they still affect judgements. It is a question of chemistry.

(b) Interviewers tend to favour candidates whose backgrounds and interests are similar to their own. Here again, these are largely emotional feelings. Candidates who went to the same school or college as the interviewers, have worked for the same employers, share the same religion or spare-time interests and activities are often subconsciously awarded plus points, which in truth have little or nothing to do with their fitness for the job.

(c) There is no uniformity in the pattern of questions nor in the interpretations of candidates' answers. These will vary from one interviewer to another.

(d) Individual interviewers will fluctuate in their judgements over a period of time. The same behaviour may be judged differently on different occasions by the same judge.

These serious deficiencies in the interview as a selection method were dramatically illustrated by an unusual experiment, carried out during World War 2 by War Office psychologists. Because of the enormous expansion of the army in wartime, a number of officer-selection boards were set up in various parts of the country. Apparently, the commanding officers of the officer-training schools, to which successful candidates were sent, drew attention to the wide variety of standards of those selected for officer-training. Without revealing their deceptive stratagem to the selectors, the War Office psychologists sent mock candidates to be assessed by a number of boards in order to test the system and to see how far varied judgements might be made about the same candidate. The results were disturbing. There was considerable fluctuation in the judgements. Candidates accepted as suitable by some boards were rejected as unsuitable by others.

In view of what we now know about the interview and the effects of human subjectivity, this is not very surprising. The experiment led to some drastic changes which have profoundly affected the process of personnel selection ever since. First, it was realized that the worst effects of human subjectivity can only be mitigated if selectors are given training which covers the problems of the interview and the need for systematic practice to use it to best effect. Secondly, it was also realized that, wherever possible, the limited evidence provided by the interview, even when skilfully conducted, needs to be supplemented by further evidence. This evidence should be as reliable and valid as possible and shown to enhance the predictive quality of the selection process by following up the subsequent performance of candidates selected by these methods. The example quoted in Chapter 4 on the problems of judgement where trainee-selectors sometimes reject mock candidates who are in fact already satisfactorily performing the jobs within the organization, is also evidence of the limitations of the selection interview. Since the interview has to be used and is sometimes the only method, every effort must be made to use the method as effectively as possible.

USING THE INTERVIEW TO BEST EFFECT

Effective interviewing is based on a systematic application of the criteria-evidence-judgement model. A systematic interview is based on three stages – before, during and after.

Before the Interview

As with all else in managerial work, preparation is vital to success. This requires the following stages:

Defining the requirements for effective performance of the criteria for judgement.

Carefully studying the application papers and noting any points that need clarification.

Preparing an interview coverage-plan.

The source of evidence likely to be the most profitable is the candidate's life-history. Notwithstanding the problems of predicting future behaviour, what people have done in the past is still the best guide to their likely future performance. The interview, therefore, is most effectively used as a systematic, chronological investigation of the life-history to reveal evidence of positive achievements, attitudes, relationship with others, etc. Since the gold may be buried in any area of the candidate's life, the coverage-plan should include the obvious main areas, i.e. education at all stages, full- and part-time, work-history and experience, training and spare-time activities. Following the investigation of the life-history, interviewers need to ask candidates to speak about the job for which they are applying, what they know about it, why they are interested in it, why they think they can perform it effectively, etc.

The closing stage of the interview plan should include two parts. First, candidates should be asked whether they wish to add anything to what has already been discussed to support their case. Hopefully, the interviewer has thoroughly covered all the necessary points. However, it is only fair to ensure that candidates have every opportunity to do themselves justice and to fill in any gaps. The interview should end with interviewers giving candidates the chance to ask any questions that they may wish to put.

Allocating time

This is especially important if a number of candidates have to be interviewed, as usually happens. Obviously there can be no fixed time for the length of a selection interview. The interview will take as long as interviewers judge to be necessary to find out what they want to know. Factors which influence the length of an interview are the complexity and importance of the job and the ages of candidates. It should normally require far more time to cover the life-history of a forty-five-year-old than that of a seventeen-year-old.

A little time must be allowed for settling into the interview and enough time afterwards to assess the evidence and make a decision. If the interview is carried out by a board of selectors, they will need to discuss the evidence and resolve any differences of opinion. If we add to this the time it is likely to take systematically and thoroughly to investigate a person's life-history, we can see that the total time required from start to finish is probably something in the region of one hour. If we bear in mind the crucial importance of the selection process and its decisions, and the serious problems that can ensue from faulty selection, one hour could hardly be regarded as an excessive amount of time to spend in assessing and deciding a candidate's suitability for several or perhaps many years of employment.

Attending to environment details

Most of what needs to be said on this subject is common sense. Obviously a quiet, comfortable place should be chosen for the interview, free from all possible distractions – telephones, builders, lawn-mowers and the like. Until fairly recent times, it was not unusual for the setting of a selection interview to be formal and forbidding, more like a courtroom. Interviewers would sit behind a table and the candidate would sit facing them at some distance. Nowadays, seating arrangements are often more relaxed so that candidates may feel more at ease and less inhibited.

Number of interviewers

Selection interviews may be conducted in three forms: one interview with one interviewer; a series of interviews with one interviewer; one interview with a board of interviewers. The board interview is the commonest form and likely to be the most effective and fair because there are several judges who can challenge and debate each other's opinions. At the same time there are some caveats that need to be borne in mind: the numbers of interviewers should be kept to the absolute minimum necessary, otherwise candidates may feel even more intimidated than they normally do; with a large number of interviewers the person in the chair has increasing difficulties of control; the person in the chair must be a very effective organizer – in the pre-interview discussion and planning stage, during the interview, and afterwards when suitability is being discussed and judgements are made.

During the Interview

To use the selection interview to best effect, it should be conducted in the following ways:

Putting candidates at ease

Bearing in mind the inherent stress of the interview situation, interviewers should do everything in their power to establish a relaxed atmosphere in which candidates feel free to talk about themselves. There is an utterly misguided belief expressed by some interviewers that candidates should be put under pressure to see how they react to this situation. Nobody who has been properly trained in selection interviewing and understands the psychology of the interview would ever dream of doing such a thing. There is enough pressure generated by the interview situation itself. But that is not the main objection, which is concerned with reliability and validity. There is no correlation between the pressures of an interview and those of work. The test is, therefore, not valid. It is not reliable because it is carried out by a variety of selectors in their own ways with no knowledge of the subject of selection tests. If ability to withstand pressure is a critical requirement, then by all means let it be tested, but only by specialists, using relevant psychometric tests of proven reliability and validity. To help candidates to relax and to talk easily, interviewers should begin by explaining the purpose and scope of the interview and then initiating an ice-breaking conversation. The conversation should cover subjects about which candidates should be able to talk easily – family, home town, etc. Once the tongue has been loosened and confidence established, the interview can move impercept-ibly into the main areas to be covered.

Following the prepared plan

This provides a map for both interviewers and candidates. The inter-viewers know where they are going and why. Candidates are able to follow the planned route. In this way, the coverage of the life-history should be comprehensive, systematic, free from gaps and productive of the maximum and best available evidence. From the candidate's point of view this approach makes recall much easier than if interviewers darted at random from one subject or one period of time to another. When the interview is carried out by a board of interviewers, the areas included in the coverage plan should be allocated to individual interviewers so that everyone knows what he or she has to do and there are no unnecessary overlaps or gaps.

Using sound questioning techniques

Ideally every question should produce relevant evidence. As we have seen when discussing the skills of asking and listening, in general the most productive questions are those which are open and free from any bias or assumptions on the part of the questioner. If we want to know somebody's age, we would naturally ask: 'How old are you?' or 'When were you born?' We would not indulge in some form of guessing game until the right answer emerged. The same principle applies to question-ing technique in general. The questions should aim to elicit as much useful information as possible about interviewees' achievements, atti-tudes and feelings. For example, when questioning about work exper-ience, interviewers would ask questions of the following kind: 'What did the job involve?' 'What were the interviewee's feelings about the job?' 'What training or other help was given?' 'What kind of problems occurred?' 'How did the candidate deal with them?' 'What did the candidate feel that he or she learned from the experience of the job?' 'Why did he or she leave the job?'

This kind of pattern of questioning should be applied to all the other areas of the life-history. All the time, the need to acquire job-related evidence should be in the forefront of interviewers' minds. Although the type of open questions described above should be used as an effective general base for the interviewers' investigation, at the same time flexibil-ity is very important. A number of questions will logically ensue from what interviewees have said. So if, for example, an interviewee says that he or she left a job because of a disagreement with the manager or dissatisfaction with working conditions, the interviewers should never let the matter rest at that point. They need to follow up such statements to find out what lies behind them. The answers may be very helpful in revealing how candidates might react in similar situations.

The point made earlier about putting information in perspective is relevant to the selection interview. If, for example, interviewees claim managerial experience, we need to know the background details of the experience: For how long did they manage? How many people did they manage? etc. As a general rule, hypothetical questions should be avoided, or at least handled with care. Hypothetical questions tend to get hypothetical answers. If we ask interviewees the 'What would you do if . . . ?' type of question, the answer does not mean that they would necessarily do in reality what they say they would do in the interview situation. If hypothetical questions are used, then certainly they ought to refer to situations and contingencies that could well arise in the job and not to some unreal fantasy.

Restricting note-taking

Note-taking in the course of an interview is obviously a potential source of discomfort and distraction for candidates. It can interrupt the flow of conversation. It breaks eye-contact whilst interviewers are writing. Candidates see that interviewers are making notes and are naturally curious about what interviewers may be recording. They may take an unnecessarily pessimistic view about what is being written. If the interview is being carried out by a board of interviewers, candidates can well be unsettled by a situation where they are answering questions from one interviewer, whilst another member of the board is busy writing. Since the comfort of candidates is of paramount importance, the wisest course is to explain to candidates at the start that occasional notes may be made, but it is not a cause for concern. Then, once the interview is under way, interviewers should keep their note-taking to a minimum and learn to write as unobtrusively as possible, using their own shorthand, and not losing eye-contact for more than a second or two. It can be done with practice.

Filling any gaps

As indicated in the broad plan, the interview should end with two questions: 'Is there anything that you think important that we have not covered?' and 'Are there any questions that you want to ask?'

After the Interview

This is the assessment phase where suitability has to be decided. Selectors must be very careful to avoid snap judgements. It is only human for selectors to start forming judgements as the interview progresses. Nevertheless, if the effects of emotions and bias are to be mitigated, interviewers must discipline themselves not to make judgements until they have gone carefully and thoroughly through the criteria and considered the evidence available.

When the interview is carried out by a board of interviewers, as it is more often than not, one of the main tasks of the person in the chair is to ensure that this disciplined, systematic approach to judgement is conscientiously carried out. Interview evidence, by its very nature, is circumstantial and needs to be considered with care and caution. As we have already seen, absence of evidence does not necessarily imply lack of ability to meet particular job requirements.

In reaching their decisions, selectors need to weigh in the balance all the evidence available to them – written documents, the interview, results of any tests that may be included in the selection process. Since the selectors' task is to judge whether candidates indicate sufficient potential to meet the requirements of a job, it may well be that more candidates pass the test of suitability than there are vacancies to be filled. In this situation, the selectors need to go very carefully through all the available evidence and credentials for each candidate, in order to place them in an order of merit. It is by no means an easy task. There may be little to choose between some candidates, and selectors may be prone to rely on hunches – not on reliable or valid means of judgement. The obvious method to adopt for distinguishing the various merits of suitable candidates is the use of weighting factors such as experience, qualifications, test results, etc.

Selection Tests

Wherever possible and practicable, interview evidence should be supplemented by any available additional evidence. A variety of tests are regularly used in the selection process, i.e. tests of ability, aptitude, intelligence, personality, behaviour in groups. Apart from tests of ability, the rest require the help of occupational psychologists to devise, monitor and validate. Tests of ability should obviously be used where jobs involve a single activity, e.g. driving, typing, playing a musical instrument, etc. It is only common sense to get candidates for employment in occupations of this kind to provide direct, measurable evidence of their proficiency.

Where psychological tests are concerned, it is easy to be seduced by the attractive possibilities of methods that will solve the problems of prediction and provide the required answers. Questions of cost-effectiveness need to be asked: e.g. 'How significantly do the tests improve the predictive value of the selection-process?' 'Are the costs involved in using tests offset by commensurate gains in reducing the number of unsound selections and hence the costs of ineffective performance?' 'How far does the importance of particular jobs justify the additional costs of tests?' For example, they might justifiably be used for the selection of pilots, but not so perhaps for the appointment of refuse collectors.

Employment Law and Employee-selection

Earlier, when job analysis was being discussed, the importance of the provisions of employment law concerning unfair discrimination was emphasized. Employee-selectors must exercise particular care during the selection process to ensure that they do not infringe the law. They need, therefore, to make sure that they know what the law says about these matters, and they they are aware of the possible pitfalls. The evidence of cases that regularly come before industrial tribunals indicates that a number of managers are still insufficiently aware of their obligations. As far as the selection process is concerned, the most likely form of any discrimination will be indirect. Here again, because of the innate bias and prejudice that human beings have, untrained employee-selectors may be unaware of these tendencies in themselves. They may not realize that it is unfair and discriminatory, for example, to ask women questions about family commitments and the effects on employability, but not to ask men similar questions. Some selection tests may be and have been contested in the courts as unfair and discriminatory because they have been shown not to have proven validity.

GUIDE NOTES FOR THE SYSTEMATIC SELECTION INTERVIEW

Aim   To obtain maximum possible job-relevant information as a basis for assessing candidate's suitability.

INTRODUCTION
- Greet candidate in friendly manner.
- Explain scope and purpose of interview, i.e. survey of life-history to assess suitability.

GENERAL BACKGROUND
- Ask candidate to give information about background – home, family, etc. (A useful ice-breaker to get candidate talking.)

EDUCATION
- What form did it take?
- What did he/she achieve academically?
- What other activities and events occurred? (e.g. extra-curricular activities).
- What did he/she gain from the experience?
- What were the plans for the future?
- What happened next and why?

WORK
- Since finishing full-time education what jobs has he/she held?
- Why did he/she take up particular jobs?
- What did they involve?
- What did he/she like/dislike about jobs? and why?
- Why did he/she leave jobs?
- What did he/she learn from the experience of jobs?

FURTHER EDUCATION AND TRAINING
- Since starting work, what further education and training has he/she undertaken?
- Why was it undertaken?
- What subjects were covered?
- What qualifications were obtained?

SPARE-TIME ACTIVITIES AND INTERESTS
- What are his/her main spare-time activities and interests?
- How did they come about?
- What do they involve?
- What does he/she gain from them?

THE JOB IN QUESTION
- What does the candidate know about the organization and the job?
- Why does he/she want the job?
- What does he/she think he/she can contribute?
- What does he/she seek to gain?
- What problems could he/she foresee?
- How might they be resolved?

CONCLUSION
- Has the interviewer missed out anything important that he/she has not had a chance to mention?
- Has he/she any questions to ask?
- Thank candidate for help. Results will be told as soon as possible.

EXERCISE ON EMPLOYEE-SELECTION

Exercise 1

- Imagine that you are vetting job-applications for a managerial post.
- Carefully study the details of one applicant on the following pages.
- Make a note of all the questions that you would want answered if you were preparing to interview this applicant.

MAIN DETAILS FROM JOB-APPLICATION FOR POST AS MANAGER OF BRANKSOME LEISURE CENTRE, POOLE, DORSET

Name	Helen Johns
Birthdate	15 May 1949
Place	Bournemouth
Present address	31 Thomas Hardy Avenue, Poole, Dorset

Education

Sept 54–Jul 60	Oakdale Junior School, Poole
Sept 60–Apr 63	Winton Comprehensive School
May 63—Jul 65	Christopher Marlow Comprehensive School, Deptford, London

Qualifications

GCE O Levels	English, Geography, Needlework, Art, Biology
RSA Certificates	Shorthand, Typing, Bookkeeping, Office Administration

Work history

Jan 66–Apr 66	Au pair, Fontainebleau, France
Jun 66–May 67	Au pair, Fontainebleau, France
Sept 67–Jul 68	Travelling in Australia
Sept 68–Jul 69	Business Studies Course at Bournemouth College of Further Education
Sept 69–Dec 76	Personal Secretary to Senior Partner of G. Higgs, Quantity Surveyors, Christchurch, Dorset
Mar 77–Aug 85	Personal Assistant to Manager, Bangers and Crocks, Automobile Co., Poole, Dorset

| Nov 85–Dec 94 | Assistant Manager, Brownsea Yacht Club and Marina, Poole, Dorset |
| **Spare-time interests and activities** | Swimming; Skittles; Darts; DIY; Reading; Travel; Pub Quizzes; Amnesty International; Graceland Society. |

CONFIDENTIAL REFERENCE FROM THE MANAGER, BANGERS AND CROCKS AUTOMOBILE CO., POOLE, DORSET

Miss Johns was employed as my P.A. from March 1978 to August 1985. In general her work was satisfactory in all respects. She is friendly and happy-go-lucky in demeanour and she got on well with the company's staff and customers. There were occasional aberrations, mainly when her children were ill and her attention was inevitably distracted.

She showed no serious faults that might detract from her ability to perform the job for which she is now applying. If she had a failing it was talkativeness. She could sometimes spend too much time gossiping to people on the telephone or to people who called in at the office.

She left this company because her partner, who was Manager of the Brownsea Yacht Club and Marina, offered her a post with a wider variety of tasks and a higher salary.

CONFIDENTIAL REFERENCE FROM THE MANAGER, BROWNSEA YACHT CLUB AND MARINA, POOLE, DORSET

Miss Johns started employment here in November 1985 as a general administrator. At that time her partner was the manager. In July 1986 she was promoted to assistant manager. She and her partner split up about a year ago when he left her to live with someone else. At the same time he left this club and moved away from this area. I became manager in December 1993 and Miss Johns has worked as my deputy since then. Since this is one of the largest clubs of its kind on the south coast, with a membership of about five hundred, the job is varied and demanding. It involves supervision of fifteen full- and part-time staff, accounting and bookkeeping, purchasing provisions and equipment, arranging for mooring and storage of some five hundred craft, organizing yachting and social events. Her performance of the job has been moderately efficient. She has a cheerful demeanour and gets on well with staff and club members. At the same time, she has a chip on her shoulder about being deserted by her former partner. This has affected her motivation. She has moods of depression, when she does not give the job the full attention it needs. A change would probably do both of us good.

QUESTIONS ARISING FROM JOB-APPLICATION DOCUMENTS

- Why did she change schools in May 1963?
- What effect did the move have?
- How many GCE (O) Levels were actually taken and with what results?
- Why did she take an au pair job in France?
- Why did she leave the first au pair job after only four months?
- Why did she decide to travel around Australia?
- What did she do in Australia?
- How did she support herself?
- Why did she decide to take a Business Studies course?
- Why did she leave Higgs, Quantity Surveyors in December 1976?
- The next job at Bangers and Crocks did not start until March 1977. What happened between December 1976 and March 1977?
- There is a discrepancy about dates of employment with Bangers and Crocks. The applicant says she started in March 1977. The referee says March 1978. Which is correct? If the referee is correct, what happened between March 1977 and 1978?
- What do the referees' reports imply – e.g. about domestic situation; circumstances of appointment and promotion in present job; present state of mind?
- Considering spare time pursuits:
    How many are still active?
    What does reading involve?
    Apart from France and Australia what travelling has she done?
    Why did she join Amnesty International?
    What does membership involve?
    What is the Graceland Society?

Exercise 2

- Produce improved forms of the following questions:
1. I suppose you left the job because you felt like a change?
2. Why did you take a course in Business Studies. Was it because you thought it might be useful for job applications?
3. Did you enjoy working in an insurance office?
4. Do you prefer work that gives job satisfaction; are you more interested in the salary, or is it perhaps the social aspects?
5. Did you pass in all the subjects of the examination?
6. No doubt you were very annoyed when you were not promoted?

SUGGESTED ANSWERS

1. *Why did you leave the job?*
2. *Why did you take a course in Business Studies? (Do not supply an answer.)*
3. *How did you feel about working in an insurance office?*
4. *What do you regard as the important things for you in a job? What do you look for when choosing a job?*
5. *How many subjects did you pass in the examination? Which ones were they?*
6. *How did you feel when you were not promoted?*

CHAPTER 7

Helping New Employees to Settle (Induction)

BASIC QUESTIONS

1 What are the problems that people starting new jobs are likely to have to face?
2 Why should managers pay particular attention to helping new employees to settle into a new job and new work-environment?
3 What should managers do to plan and provide an effective induction programme?

Once candidates for employment have successfully passed through the selection process and have become employees of a work organization, they face a difficult period of time settling into the new job and into the employing organization as a whole. Even existing employees moving within the organization from one job to another have a similar problem in settling down anew. However, having been already employed in the organization, they are at least familiar with its culture and environment.

Induction can be defined as the period in which new employees adapt and become integrated into a new environment, which involves the work-group to which they have been allocated and the organization as a whole. The process of induction includes professional, social and psychological aspects. Newcomers not only have to learn to become technically effective in the performance of their jobs, they also have to be able to work co-operatively with their colleagues and to become committed members of the employing organization. Induction is not something swiftly completed. It may take several months before newcomers really feel at home.

All human beings face difficulties when joining new groups at school, college, work, etc. The feelings of uncertainty inevitably affect people of all ages and experience. The very experienced senior manager moving to a new job still has to adjust to new surroundings. Newcomers have no history or reputation in the new appointment. They may bring some reputation from former jobs, but no matter what that may be, they still have to start again and prove their worth afresh.

The evidence of research indicates that the induction phase of employment and its attendant problems have not always received the understanding and careful attention that is really needed. Newly appointed employers can easily be demotivated if they do not get the help they need from their managers to settle into the new environment and to overcome any stress that the so-called induction crisis may cause.

The fact that all people find some difficulties of adjustment when settling into a new job does not sound like a startling revelation. It could be dismissed as something that is self-evident. Furthermore, since it is an experience that all human beings share at some time in their lives, managers could be expected to understand the problems and to have some empathy with newcomers. No doubt they generally do, but they may also forget just how stressful the experience can be and thus fail to do everything possible and necessary to give all the help that people may need. It is certainly not enough to regard the induction phase as a temporary discomfort which time will cure. Managers need to look beyond the obvious conclusions about the induction crisis. They also need to understand fully the nature of the induction phase and its problems. What are the causes of the induction crisis?

1. New employees are in a position of insecurity. The continuity of their working lives has been broken by the change of jobs or they may be starting work for the first time, in which case feelings of unease, uncertainty and strangeness are likely to be even stronger. They have no previous history in the new job. They may or may not bring some kind of reputation with them to the new situation, but achievements in the past count for little at the start of a new job. People have to prove that they are effective in professional and social terms, and that takes time.

2. Norms have already been mentioned in the discussion of group behaviour. Newcomers have to learn over time what the particular

characteristics are of a new work-group and a new employing organization.

3. New employees will have learned something about the employing organization through published literature and the selection process. Reality may be different and give rise to disappointment. An American psychologist, H. Levinson, has proposed the concept of a 'psychological contract'. Employees have expectations of economic rewards from the employer which are clearly defined in the contract of employment. Levinson suggests that there is also a 'psychological contract' which is not made explicit, but which exists all the same. It refers to expectations that employees have about the way the employer should treat them in human terms. The style of management could cause problems, for example, if the employee, expecting a democratic-participative style, is in fact subjected to authoritarian management. What can managers do to mitigate any adverse effects that the induction phase may have on new employees?

(a) They need to understand the nature and causes of problems and be fully aware of the importance of a good start to a new career as a motivating force.

(b) They need to produce and implement a broad general plan which can be adapted in its details to suit individual needs. The first step in the induction plan is to define its aim and objectives, as follows.

Aim
To integrate new employees into their new jobs and new organization functionally, socially and psychologically as soon as possible.

Objectives
New employees should know:

  (i) the aim, objectives and functions of the employing organization;

 (ii) the specific objectives of their own work-group and how they relate to the organizational aim and objectives;

(iii) the requirements for effective performance of their own jobs, as described in the job-description and person specification;

(iv) the system of performance appraisal and the requirements for them to assess their own performance;

 (v) the details of their contracts of employment;

(vi) the provisions for personnel functions such as welfare, health and safety, complaints, discipline;

(vii) the availability of staff to answer questions or deal with problems during the induction phase;

(viii) the details of their own induction programmes and the arrangements for monitoring its effectiveness.

In collaboration with the personnel staff, managers are responsible for implementing the induction programme and for monitoring its effectiveness. The programme should include interviews, training, work experience and provisions for social adaptation as described below.

Induction Interviews

It may be that managers and new employees have already met during the selection process. Sometimes the induction interview is the first meeting. The aim of the interview is to make newcomers feel welcome and reassured. It will involve gathering and giving information and should cover the following points:

1. Welcome and brief explanation of the purpose and scope of the interview.
2. Brief account by the new employee of his/her career to date, interests and any problems that managers need to know (e.g. invalid wife/ husband), together with thoughts about the new job. This information will be recorded on the employee's application form and may also have been heard by the manager during the selection interview. Nevertheless, a brief rehearsal of the main facts of the employee's background and career history will remind managers. It will also give new employees a chance to talk and ensure that the employee is not subjected to a managerial monologue.
3. Manager's account of all the areas of information covered by the objectives.
4. Invitation to the employee to raise any questions.

There seems to be so much that people need to know when they join new work-groups that there is always the danger of burying them under a mass of information. Managers have to remember that there are limits to the amount of information and advice that new employees can absorb at one time. The purpose of the interview is to help and reassure, but not to bewilder. It is not essential to cram everything into one interview. Parts of the information to be covered could usefully be delegated to a senior member of the work-group. Some information could be provided as a written hand-out for new employees to read at leisure.

Training

People starting at a new job will more often than not need some form of training. Sometimes this is mandatory, centrally directed and provided. For example, all newly recruited policemen have to undergo a basic training course to provide them with an essential basis before they start their operational duties. Training may take the form of short full-time courses or of much longer programmes, where a high level of perform-ance is required, e.g. flying training, engineering apprenticeship, etc.

Apart from any mandatory, centrally directed training, newcomers may have training needs that apply only to themselves. For example, the job description may require the job-holder regularly to chair meetings. If the new job-holder has had little or no experience of this task, a training course might be necessary to provide the basic framework needed for effective performance. It is the responsibility of managers to identify individual training needs of this kind and to prescribe the appropriate form of training. The National and Local Government Officers Associ-ation (NALGO), introduced some years ago, a very effective scheme for assessing the training needs of new employees. The scheme ensures standardized practice by all managers in the organization. The scheme is based on two interviews in addition to the main induction interview. Its main details are described below:

1. At the main induction interview, managers explain the scheme and give new employees a Training Needs Assessment form (TNA 2) to help them assess their own needs. This is done by reference to a Training Profile which describes in detail the knowledge and skills required for each task of the job.
2. With reference to the employee's application form for appointment, notes made during the selection procedure and the same training profile, managers make their own assessments of the new employee's training needs (TNA 1).
3. After a week or two, managers and employees meet to discuss and compare their views and eventually to agree on the training needs.
4. Managers then spend whatever time is required to deliberate and decide how best the identified training needs might be met (TNA 3).

5. Managers and employees then meet for a second time to discuss the training to be recommended.

Specimen forms TNA 1, 2 and 3 and a Training Profile are appended at the end of the chapter.

Work Experience

Important and necessary though training always is, there is no substitute for the learning gained from the direct experience of work. A well-known and proven method is to place a newcomer under the tutelage of an experienced employee. It used to be known for some obscure reason as 'sitting by Nelly'. In the USA it is called 'the buddy system'. Clearly the choice of 'Nelly' is very important. Managers should be extremely careful in their choice of these tutors. They need to be reliable, trustworthy, professionally competent members of staff, who will not only supervise the newcomer's work in the early days, but will also act as guardian, mentor, counsellor and friend. People chosen for this extremely important role should set a good example. Example is a powerful learning medium especially for younger employees who may be starting their very first jobs. 'Nelly' should be somebody who not only possesses the abilities and qualities described above, but is also a committed member of the organization. Good influences in the early stages of a work career can have long-lasting effects.

There are other useful methods of helping new employees to develop into effective performers of their jobs. The induction programme might include the following forms of on-job learning:

1. **Coaching**. A form of one-to-one training. There is an analogy here with sport, where the tennis coach, for example, will concentrate on particular aspects of the game, i.e. serving, volleying, etc. In a similar way, the work-coach concentrates on particular aspects of jobs in which the job-holder needs special help.
2. **Job-rotation**. If job-holders need to have knowledge of other jobs in the group in order to perform their own jobs effectively, managers can arrange for them to spend some time working alongside other colleagues in turn, in order to gain the required knowledge through direct experience.
3. **Visits and attachments**. Sometimes jobs require knowledge of and involvement with other units in the organization. Here again, direct

experience can be invaluable. If this is so, then the induction programme should make provisions for new employees to visit or to be
attached for a short period to these units. This kind of experience can
enhance work performance considerably and avoid misunderstandings. For example, how much more effective the civilian lecturer
at the police training school is likely to be if he or she has spent some
time visiting and being attached to operational police units to learn
about police work firsthand. This is a practical example of using shared
experience to develop communication.

Visits and attachments should be structured as a planned, learning
experience. New employees should not be sent off casually to visit other
work locations to see what they can find out. The managers of the
receiving units need to be involved, to be given details of the employees,
the purposes of the visit and what they need to know. Visits should be
followed up with a debriefing involving managers and the new
employees to assess the value and to deal with any questions arising.

Here is an example that illustrates the potential benefits of visits and
attachments for employees whose jobs require regular external contacts.
Miss X was a clerk, working at the HQ of a large organization with
subsidiary units located in various parts of the country. Her work was
concerned with correspondence with these units by letter and regularly
by telephone. A newly appointed manager discovered that, although she
had been corresponding with these units for several years, she had little
idea about what they did or of the value and significance of her work to
them. The new manager planned for her to visit a representative sample
of these units for a day at a time to meet her hitherto invisible correspond-
ents face-to-face to learn more about what they did and how she could
make her service to them more useful. The benefits were soon obvious.
Improved communication led to more effective performance; but more
than that the morale and motivation of this clerk improved visibly. The
visits should have been planned and made ages ago, during the induction
phase of new employment.

Whatever methods for work-experience are chosen will depend on the
nature of particular jobs. The criteria for choice of methods will be
determined by what job-holders need to know and how best they can
acquire the necessary knowledge. Managers need to develop a range of
options and, above all, to show imagination and creativity in their choice
and use.

Social Adaptation

This is the most difficult part of the induction phase because of its psychological implications. Managers cannot be expected to be aware of all the psychological nuances and undercurrents that characterize intra-group relationships. They need to know the members of their groups for all the reasons related to effective performance, and the induction of new employees is one of these. This is why the democratic-participative style of management is potentially the most effective. If managers get out and about with their eyes and ears open, they can anticipate how the social forces of the work-group could affect new employees, how they might be used to advantage and how they might cause problems. To take a commonly occurring example, new employees, and especially the young and inexperienced, may sometimes have to be protected from well-known disgruntled members of a group, who latch on to newcomers to pour out their woes. The more members of the group that the manager can involve in helping newcomers to feel at home the better.

The complexity, duration and individuality of the induction phase needs to be fully appreciated. The process of adapting to a new society in professional, social and psychological terms is subtle and inevitably varies for each individual. Whilst new employees may go through some parts of an induction programme as a group, the time required for each individual to cross the line that separates novitiates from integrated employees may vary considerably with each individual employee. So, as well as group induction programmes, managers must always be alert to the needs of individuals and plan their induction accordingly. Undoubtedly, this does require care and time, but in terms of effective, committed employees the rewards can be invaluable.

Finally, the induction of new employees is the first stage in their development discussed in detail in Chapter 9. It begins as soon as they cross the threshold of employment.

NALGO TRAINING NEEDS ASSESSMENT SCHEME FOR NEW EMPLOYEES

TRAINING PROFILE FOR ADMINISTRATIVE OFFICERS IN DISTRICTS

Function	Knowledge	Skills
1 Functions as an effective member of NALGO staff.	1.1 Has a working knowledge of NALGO structure, including: – NALGO Constitution and Rules – District Council Rules and Procedures – HQ services – negotiating machinery – policy-making procedures. Understands the role of the district office and his/her own role in relation to it. Has a sound general understanding of the structure and working of the Trade Union movement.	
2 Deals with telephone enquiries over the whole range of the Association's activities.	2.1 Deals with general enquiries appropriate to his/her level of knowledge and responsibilities. 2.2 Refers other telephone enquiries to the appropriate NALGO officer/external source, or takes messages as appropriate.	2.3 Speaks on the telephone in a clear and pleasant voice. 2.4 Conveys information clearly and concisely. 2.5 Extracts relevant information from callers speedily and courteously.
3 Corresponds with – NALGO HQ, Branches and individual members – Official bodies (including local authorities; government departments) – Suppliers and contractors.	3.1 Drafts letters in a format conforming to district office practice. 3.2 Follows best business practice in letters relating to purchases and contracts.	3.3 Writes clear and concise English.
4 Acts as manager of the clerical and typing staff in the district office.	4.1 Has working knowledge of the NALGO Staff Regulations, and a detailed knowledge of those concerning salaries and conditions of service of clerical and typing staff, including relevant welfare provisions.	4.3 Monitors and controls the exercise of supervisory functions delegated to clerical or typing supervisors.

Function	Knowledge	Skills
	4.2 Has thorough knowledge of regulations and procedures governing: – selection and recruitment of staff – grievance handling – disciplinary action – appeals (including grading appeals) – new technology.	4.4 Successfully maintains discipline and motivation of staff under his/her control. Adopts appropriate and effective interview techniques in relation to: – selection interviews – disciplinary interviews – counselling/grievance interviews. 4.5 Gives clear and concise instructions in clerical procedures and office routine.
5. Exercises certain personnel functions in respect of Branch Organisers and Branch Administrators, including: – participating in induction training of newly appointed staff in respect of District Office organization and procedures – monitoring sickness, leave and other absence.	5.1 Has working knowledge of the particular conditions of service of Branch Organizers and Branch Administrators, and of their functions and responsibilities in relation to District Office.	5.2 Gives clear and concise instruction in relevant aspects of District Office organisation and procedures. 5.3 Keeps accurate clear and up-to-date records of sickness, leave and other absences of BOs and BAs.
6 Oversees and co-ordinates the administrative activities of the district office (including special responsibility for maintenance and security of premises, and for letting of committee rooms where appropriate).	6.1 Thorough knowledge and understanding of the rules and procedures operating in the district office, relating to: – correspondence (including typing) – filing and record systems – equipment and stationery – simple financial procedures (including estimates and cash handling) – general housekeeping (including maintenance, security and health and safety) – letting of committee rooms. 6.2 Has an awareness and understanding of recommended best practices in office management, maintenance and security, and suggests improved procedures where appropriate.	6.3 Understands and practises appropriate management techniques of: – planning and allocation of work – co-ordination – delegation – monitoring. 6.4 Keeps accurate and clear records of lettings of committee rooms.

Function	Knowledge	Skills
7 Operates specific procedures relating to NALGO membership rules and election.	7.1 Thorough knowledge of the procedures governing: – Branch annual membership returns – District Council meetings – District Council elections – NEC elections – TUC elections – Bridlington agreement.	7.2 Maintains records and carries out administrative procedures with meticulous accuracy.
8 Provides all necessary administrative services to the District Council, District Service Conditions Committees, etc.	8.1 Understands the rules and procedures governing committee meetings, especially: – agendas and notice of meetings – minutes – follow-up action – special practice and procedures governing meetings of committees to which he/she is specially attached.	8.2 Takes clear and exact notes of significant points raised in discussion, and of all decisions taken. 8.3 Writes clear and concise English.
9 Acts as treasurer of specific district financial accounts as required.	9.1 Has working knowledge of regulations and procedures governing the administration of the funds for which he/she is responsible.	9.2 Keeps meticulous account of all moneys entrusted to his/her charge in a manner conforming to relevant regulations and accepted best practice.
10 Prepares reports and briefing documents for DOO, on personnel matters, equipment, etc.	10.1 Drafts reports in a format conforming to the district office practice.	10.2 Assimilates written information readily and selects items relevant to the matter in hand. 10.3 Writes clear and concise English. 10.4 Assembles material into a clear and logical sequence.
11 Makes accommodation and travel arrangements for NALGO members and staff attending district and national functions, e.g. council and committee meetings.	11.1 Keeps up-to-date records of suitable hotel and college accommodation in the district, and appropriate public transport facilities. 11.2 Has a thorough knowledge of the NALGO Regulations governing travelling and subsistence expenses, and the procedures for payment and reimbursement.	

Function	Knowledge	Skills
12. Organizes despatch of committee papers, circulars and other documents to members of the District Council, district committees and to branches.	12.1 Keeps complete and up-to-date records of branch officers, District Council members and other appropriate addressees. 12.2 Knows of alternative sources of essential services (especially printing).	12.3 Establishes and operates effective routines for the production, collation, packing and despatch of material.
13 Oversees the administration of the district office branch.	13.1 Has a working knowledge of the procedures relating to the district office branch.	

Form TNA.I

NALGO STAFF TRAINING
TRAINING NEEDS ASSESSMENT INTERVIEW

Manager's Preparation Form

Name of employee	Designation of Post

The purpose of this form is to assist you in preparing for a Training Needs Assessment Interview with the member of staff named above. It is intended to assist you in two ways: first, to focus your thinking prior to the interview, and secondly to serve as a memory prompter during the interview itself. You may find it helpful to write down your answers to each question in the space provided. You may also find it helpful to add to the appropriate section of the form a note of any additional training needs or proposals that may come to light during the interview itself. Before attempting to answer the questions on this form you should first read through the job description and training profile for the employee's post, and any other relevant papers that you may have available, such as his/her application form for the post, and/or any notes taken at his/her selection interview.

Question I
Which of the duties listed in the employee's job description/training profile does it appear that the employee has already performed or is likely to be familiar with?

_____

_____

_____

_____

_____

_____

Question 2

(a) Are there any of the duties that you have listed under Question I where the employee is likely to need further training or experience?

(b) What types of training activity would be most appropriate to meet those needs?

Question 3

Now consider the remaining duties listed on the employee's job description/training profile (i.e. those s/he has not yet performed).

(a) In which of these does it appear likely, from your knowledge of the employee and of the job, that there will be a training need?

(b) What types of training activity would be most appropriate to meet those needs?

_____

_____

_____

_____

_____

_____

Question 4

Turning to the training profile for the employee's post, and in particular at the column headed 'Needs to know' and 'Needs to do':

(a) Are there any other areas of knowledge or skill listed there where you feel the employee is likely to have a training need?

(b) What sources of information or types of training activity are available to meet these needs?

_____

_____

_____

_____

_____

Form TNA.2

NALGO STAFF TRAINING
TRAINING NEEDS ASSESSMENT INTERVIEW

Employee's Preparation Form

Please study carefully the job description and training profile for your post. NALGO accepts that nobody comes into a new post completely equipped in every way to perform its duties. Everybody can benefit from training in some area or another. At the Training Needs Assessment Interview you and your manager will discuss together your training needs with a view to producing a suitable training and development programme suited to your individual needs.

This form is for your personal use in preparing for the interview. You will not be required to hand it in. However, please go through it carefully, and note down your answers to each of the questions. Then bring it with you to the interview. You will find it a useful memory prompter when you are discussing your training needs with your manager.

Question 1

Which of the duties listed in your job description/training profile have you already performed, either in this post or in a previous one?

_____

_____

_____

_____

_____

_____

Question 2

Of the duties you have listed under Question 1, for which if any do you feel that you have a need for further training or experience?

_____

_____

_____

_____

_____

_____

Question 3

Now consider the other duties on your job description/training profile, i.e. those you have not yet performed. For which, if any, of them do you feel that you have particular training needs?

_____

_____

_____

_____

_____

_____

Question 4

Now look at your training profile and in particular look at the columns headed 'Needs to know' and 'Needs to do'. Are there any other areas of knowledge or skill listed there where you feel that you may need training?

_____

_____

_____

_____

_____

_____

Question 5

Is there anything else at all, relevant to your future training, that you would like to discuss with your manager?

_____

_____

_____

_____

_____

_____

Form TNA.3

TRAINING RECOMMENDATION FORM

Name of Employee	District/Department	Designation

I conducted a Training Needs Assessment Interview with the above member of

staff on_____, and recommend that s/he
undertakes the training activities indicated below.

Signed_____ Date_____

I agree the contents of this form:

Signed_____ Date_____

(Employee)

Note: In the appropriate column of section (ii) please enter one of the following code letters to indicate the degree of urgency:

X – Immediate (needed at once)
S – Short-term (needed within the next 3 months)
M – Medium-term (needed within the next year)
L – Long-term

This section to be filled in when recommended training has been completed

No.	(i) Area of training need	(ii) Recommended method of meeting need						(iii) Specific coach/ref. material/ visit/course/qualification recommended	(iv) Training provided	(v) Date completed
		Coaching on the job	Reference material	Visits	Short courses	Qualifications	Other			
		A	B	C	D	E	F			
1.										
2.										
3.										

No.	(i) Area of training need	(ii) Recommended method of meeting need						(iii) Specific coach/ref. material/visit/course/qualification recommended	(iv) Training provided	(v) Date completed
		A Coaching on the job	B Reference material	C Visits	D Short courses	E Qualifications	F Other			
4.										
5.										
6.										
7.										
8.										
9.										
10.										
11.										
12.										

EXERCISE ON INDUCTION OF NEW EMPLOYEES

- Refer to the plan for an induction programme described in this chapter.
- Produce a comprehensive plan, based on this programme, to be used for an employee newly appointed to your work-group.

CHAPTER 8

Performance-Appraisal

BASIC QUESTIONS

1 What is the importance of performance-appraisal in the management of people?
2 What should its objectives be?
3 How should the objectives affect the details of performance-appraisal schemes in practice?
4 What are the main requirements for an effective system of performance-appraisal?

When the criteria-evidence-judgement model is applied to performance-appraisal, job analysis defines the criteria, performance-appraisal provides the evidence and judgement. Its obvious aim is to determine whether the criteria defined for effective performance are being met and what action needs to be taken. It is axiomatic that the effective performance of work can only be achieved on this basis. Nevertheless, there is a history of protest about performance-appraisal by employees. Whether the protesters have realized it or not, their objections have not, in fact, been directed against performance-appraisal *per se*. They have been directed against managerial, confidential systems based on a Theory X philosophy of management. The protests have been fully justified.

This book is based on a belief that the development of an organization's human resources is of crucial importance to the effectiveness of the organization and to the commitment, motivation and contentment of its employees. This goal is most likely to be achieved by a democratic, Theory Y approach to management. It determines the kind of performance-appraisal system that all organizations need to have, if they believe that the development and welfare of the employees is important. If you want to know what an organization truly believes about the treatment of its employees – never mind what it says it believes – look at its system of performance appraisal. 'By their deeds ye shall know them.'

Since the details of a performance-appraisal scheme are a logical consequence of purpose, it is necessary to start with a comprehensive definition of objectives, as described below. Theory Y schemes that emphasize the development of employees will be based on objectives of the following kind.

Specific Objectives

- To review the criteria for effective performance (i.e. job description and person specification) and to revise them, if circumstances have changed. There is no point in assessing the evidence of performance in terms of requirements that are no longer valid.
- To ascertain whether any changes are needed in conditions of work, e.g. methods, accommodation, equipment, etc. and to find appropriate remedies.
- To assess the performance of employees in terms of the defined criteria; to identify strengths and weaknesses; to decide what future action and help may be needed, e.g. further work experience, training, etc.
- To assess the effectiveness of measures already taken as a result of previous appraisals of performance, i.e. have they had the intended effect on subsequent work performance?

General Objectives

- To give employees advice and help in improving performance and dealing with personal problems as necessary.
- To develop employees' commitment towards their jobs, groups and employing organizations.
- To develop versatility.
- To develop self-reliance, the ability to assess self, one's own performance and behaviour, and to solve one's own problems.
- To foster productive relationships between managers and their staffs.

The authoritarian, confidential, Theory X approach to performance-appraisal has now largely passed into history, although some vestiges still persist. Contemporary practice reflects the development in recent times of more democratic-participative styles of management. As a result of these changes performance-appraisal tends to be based on objectives similar to those described above. Having defined our objectives, we can now consider the details of a performance-appraisal scheme that would enable these objectives to be met.

The first conclusion affecting actual practice that emerges from the objectives is that the appraisal must be carried out on an open, joint, participative basis. Without a frank discussion between managers and the people whose performance is being appraised, the objectives cannot be met. It also makes sense psychologically to allow and to encourage those who are being appraised to have their say, to contribute to decisions affecting them personally and to have a chance of influencing their manager's views and proposals. If Peter Drucker is right in arguing that debated opinions are likely to lead to better decisions than those produced unilaterally, then a two-way discussion should produce better results than a managerial monologue. It would doubtless go against the grain with old-fashioned, authoritarian managers to give their subordinates so much rope. How else can people be encouraged to think for themselves, to solve their own problems and to learn what to do without spoon feeding? Far from being a sign of weakness, it needs strength, self-confidence, intelligence, sensitivity and interpersonal skills for managers to be able to tolerate views from subordinates which are contrary to their own. It is a sign of maturity if managers are prepared to change their minds when faced with convincing arguments. When considering interpersonal skills in Chapter 3, the importance of listening and its relevance to effective management was emphasized. It is not a skill which people find easy. Managers need to heed what the individual members of their groups think and feel, to consider whether their thoughts and feelings seem to be justified and reasonable, or whether they have got hold of the wrong end of the stick. As we have already seen, human communication is bedevilled by false assumptions and misunderstandings. Performance-appraisal discussions, if effectively conducted, can help to unravel these communicational knots, but only if managers ask open, pertinent questions and listen carefully to what people say. It cannot be done if managers insist on a right to do all the talking and telling. In any case, at the end of the day, managers still have to make the final decision, whatever people being appraised may say. They have to decide – are we going to do this your way or my way?

The next point to be made concerns timing. Ask anyone about performance-appraisal and the chances are that he or she will think in terms of a periodic review. For most people it means an annual appraisal and report.

Undoubtedly, it is important to the cause of effective management to stand back from the daily round, to take stock of achievement, to see the wood for the trees, and to make plans for the future. At the same time it is surely necessary to keep an eye on the ball all the time, to be continually assessing progress and to take immediate remedial action, whenever necessary. Problems and needs can arise at any time. Action is often necessary here and now. We cannot wait, say, for several months until the next formal appraisal becomes due.

It follows logically, therefore, that in addition to periodic reviews, managers and their staffs need to hold appraisal discussions at regular intervals. How often these should be held is a matter for managers to decide for themselves. Anyway, they need to draw up a schedule for discussions to be held individually with every member of their teams say, for example, every three months. The schedule should also include provisions for meetings and discussions at any other times if a particular matter requires urgent attention. Whilst these discussions should be conducted in a very informal atmosphere, it is important that managers adhere to the schedule and meet the members of their staffs at fixed dates and times. If they are held casually as and when they can be fitted into the busy and sometimes frantic timetable of work, we all know what is likely to happen. Discussions will be postponed or even cancelled because other supposedly more important matters have cropped up. Few things, if any, are more important than regularly appraising work as a means of achieving effective performance, not to mention its motivational and communicational purposes.

Any assessment of the performance of work has to be based on actual examples and not impressions. Concrete evidence is necessary to support any views that managers or individuals being assessed may wish to make. There is only one way to be sure that the evidence is as sound as it can be, and that is to keep records. In the intervals between one meeting and the next, both managers and members of their work-group should make notes of any matters that need to be raised. Of course, people are usually too busy to be able to spend much time keeping expansive work-diaries. It is not suggested in any way that they should do any more than jot down relevant points as they occur, which should not require more than a few minutes of their time.

Apart from the fact that routine discussions of this kind should be a very important part of any good manager's job, they have some significant benefits as part of the whole system of performance-appraisal:

1. **They complement the periodic review**. If managers and their staffs have been involved in regular discussions throughout the year, then the periodic review becomes a summary of the routine, regular discussions. The important groundwork will have already been covered and the periodic review is no longer the annual ritual – or even ordeal – that it is in some organizations.

2. **They solve the memory problem**. A well-known problem that regularly affects periodic reviews, especially those held annually, is recall. It is very difficult for people to remember accurately events that happened, say, eleven months ago. The memory is inevitably focused on the recent past. Facetiously speaking, we could advise employees whose work-performance is assessed only once every year to put the best foot forward in the weeks preceding the review, and above all to avoid any behaviour that might blot the copy-book. If managers and their staffs have been meeting throughout the year for regular, routine discussions and accumulating evidence based on recorded notes, the problem of memory and accuracy is largely resolved.

3. **They help communication**. When the appraisal of work-performance is based on the annual ritual, it could well be that managers and individual employees have misunderstandings about what each wants, thinks and feels. This could become serious, if allowed to fester unchecked for months on end. It is not unknown, even when periodic reviews are based on open, joint discussions, for some surprises and occasional shocks to occur, simply through a lack of communication. Examples of the 'I think that you think that I . . .' syndrome may occur.

    Here is an actual example. An employee, having recently been appraised by his line-manager, expressed misgivings to the counter-signing manager (the superior manager of the line-manager). He said that he believed that his line-manager disapproved of him, because they were regularly involved in arguments, in which the employee in question sometimes strongly disagreed with the line-manager. He thought, therefore, that the line-manager regarded him as insubordinate and troublesome and had probably reported on him adversely. The counter-signing manager, who naturally had seen and commented on the line-manager's report, which, incidentally, was confidential, reassured the unhappy employee. He told him that he had completely misunderstood the situation. In fact, the line-manager had praised him for thinking constructively about his work and for being frank and honest in voicing his opinions. The problem would probably not have occurred had they discussed work more regularly and learned to communicate feelings.

Having established that regular, joint discussions based on recorded notes is the basis of an effective system, we can now examine how the system should work in practice.

The Induction Interview

The induction interview is the first step in the performance-appraisal system. Managers need to take the following steps:

1. Go through the job description and person specification with new employees so that they fully understand what they are required to do and what the criteria are by which the performance of their work will be judged.
2. Explain the details of the system, i.e.:
   (a) It is a joint-participative system which requires job-holders to assess their own performance.
   (b) Managers and employees will meet regularly for scheduled discussions (e.g. every three months).
   (c) The broad agenda for performance-appraisal discussions will be:
      (i) the job – are there any problems (e.g. methods, equipment, accommodation, etc.)?; are any changes needed in the job description or person specification?;
      (ii) performance – are job-holders meeting the specified requirements of the job. If not, why not? What action needs to be taken, what help do they need?
   (d) Apart from scheduled discussions, both line-managers and job-holders should make brief notes about agenda items to be used as *aide-memoires* during regular discussions and to provide work-related examples to support any views or conclusions.

Scheduled Discussions

Managers and job-holders meet according to the schedule to discuss the job and its performance, using the notes that each has made. Managers should then make a brief record of the meeting, which gives a brief account of subjects discussed, points raised and decisions. A copy should be given to the job-holders.

The Periodic Review

These reviews are held annually more often than not. They could well be held more regularly, e.g. every six months, if that is what a particular organization wishes. The review has three stages – preparation; the review discussion; report of the discussion; the details of which are described below. In essence this review is not very different from the regular scheduled discussions. The main difference is the scope of the review. Covering the same agenda, i.e. the job, performance and action required, this review embraces the whole job. Managers and individual employees assess progress over a longer period, assess the achievement of the objective of the job, review objectives and plan for the future.

Preparation and Assessment

Managers arrange a mutually convenient date, time and place. The time should allow the review to take as long as is necessary. It cannot be satisfactorily carried out if managers have one eye on the clock. The venue should be quiet and free from interruptions. Despite the protection that personal secretaries might give, managers' offices may not always be the best place. The details of the agenda and preparation for assessment need to be discussed. Having had regular meetings with their managers throughout the year, job-holders should now know very well what the review involves and what they are required to contribute. It should certainly not be anything like the ordeal that it sometimes is, when managers and job-holders meet only once a year. In accordance with the policy of joint, participative appraisal, during the preparation period managers and job-holders make their separate assessments to be compared and discussed during the review itself. In preparing for the review-discussion, managers and job-holders will naturally refer to notes that have been made throughout the review period as a result of regular, scheduled discussions. All periodic performance-appraisal reviews are based on forms designed to guide assessors and to standardize practice throughout the organization. The kind of form that is required for this review is an extension of the philosophy and practice of the system. It must reflect the principles of systematic judgement based on a definition of criteria and the accumulation of valid evidence. The items included in the form should compel the discipline of systematic judgement. How far the purpose of the job has been achieved will depend on how effectively the component tasks have been carried out. In preparing for the review discussion, managers and job-holders should work separately through the items of the form, considering each task in turn, producing evidence of performance, and finally drawing conclusions about effectiveness of performance and any action needed. Organizations naturally have their own preferences for the format of performance-appraisal forms. However, in order to ensure a systematic analysis of each component task the form should include the following headings. It is completed by managers and staff being appraised.

1.	2.	3.
Task	*Evidence*	*Conclusions*

Column 1 will list the component tasks as defined in the job description.
Column 2 will be used to cite evidence of actual performance.
Column 3 will be used for noting conclusions about the performance of each task.

Achievement of Purpose

In this section both assessors will assess how far the purpose of the job has been achieved in the light of the assessments of the component tasks.

Future Action Proposed

In this section both assessors will list the action that they consider necessary to improve the job and to develop the job-holder.

Discussion and Comparison of Views

Managers and job-holders meet to discuss and compare views using the forms which both have completed. As agreed, they discuss the job, performance, action and plans for the future. Managers are 'in the chair' and should always ask job-holders to speak first. As a technique this approach has the following considerable advantages:

1. It gives job-holders confidence that their views are being listened to and heeded and that the discussion is not a managerial monologue.
2. It alerts managers to any differences of views between themselves and job-holders.
3. Becoming aware of any differences, managers can then explore the reasons and attempt to resolve the problem.

Managers will start the discussion by considering the job itself, asking job-holders whether they wish to make any comments or suggestions about the job description, conditions of work, methods, etc. The next item on the agenda will be the performance of the job. Using the form that both have completed, managers discuss each task in turn, asking job-holders to produce the evidence and conclusions they have reached. Listening to what job-holders have to say, managers can agree or disagree. If they disagree they will need to explore reasons for disagreement. Do they agree about evidence of performance? If not, why not? Finally, they need to summarize conclusions and the action required to be taken to make any necessary changes, to remedy any weaknesses and to develop the people whose work is being appraised. A detailed example is appended at the end of the chapter.

Report on Performance-appraisal Review

The performance-appraisal review is a meeting between the manager and an individual member of his or her work-group. Since it is a meeting with specific purposes for future action, it needs to be recorded. At the final stage of the review, managers should, therefore, produce a brief record to show what was discussed, what was agreed and not agreed, and what action was proposed for the future. A copy of this record should then be passed to the individual concerned so that he or she may be satisfied of its accuracy and is able to retain a copy for future reference.

The approach to performance-appraisal described in this chapter has the following virtues:

1. It is systematic, being based on a criteria-evidence-judgement method.
2. It is based on regular discussions about work and performance.
3. It requires assessors to assess the important tasks of the jobs.
4. It concentrates on the improvement of performance and development of employees.
5. It involves job-holders throughout in assessing their own performance and participating in their own development. This ought, therefore, to be a motivating factor.

A number of organizations still use performance-appraisal systems which require managers to give marks for a list of traits, e.g. reliability, initiative. These systems originated in the public sector – the Civil Service and the armed forces. They are also used in a number of overseas

countries which were formerly British colonies. It is worth saying something about this form of appraisal, first to show how fundamentally
flawed it is, and secondly to show how the method recommended in this
chapter can and should be adapted for use within a traits-numbers
system.

The weaknesses of the traits-numbers system are these:

1. Assessors may well have differing interpretations of the various traits.
2. Lists of traits needed for effective performance could be extremely
   lengthy.
3. The personal qualities defined as necessary for effective performance
   are undoubtedly very important. But in the end the only important
   questions are – have employees effectively performed the tasks of the
   job? What is the actual evidence of performance?
4. To be required to assess whether employees have shown initiative
   requires the assessors to consider all the separate tasks of the job
   together.
5. Assessors required to give marks for traits are free to give whatever
   marks they wish without any requirement to substantiate their assessments with valid evidence. The system is, therefore, inherently unfair.
6. Many assessors seldom, if ever, give full marks because they regard
   this as indicating absolute perfection. However, if they give an
   employee, say, 4 out of 5 for reliability, they cannot avoid the obvious
   conclusion that the employee is not fully reliable. It is fairly certain that
   they would not be able to cite valid evidence of any unreliability. One
   very well-known organization included loyalty in its list of traits. To
   give an employee 4 out of 5 would have been considered a very
   favourable assessment by many managers. Looked at another way, it
   would also mean that employees given this mark were only four-fifths
   loyal, whatever loyalty is considered to mean.

Managers who are saddled with a performance-appraisal system of this
kind can and indeed should carry out their appraisal by taking each task
in turn and carefully considering the evidence. When they have done this,
they can then consider marks for traits, which at least will be based on a
careful analysis of the actual performance of the tasks of the job.

Systems are only as good as the people who use them. Performance-
appraisal requires considerable interpersonal and communicational skills
on the part of the manager. It also needs tolerance, maturity and sometimes magnanimity. If employees are encouraged to assess themselves
and to say what they think and feel, then the manager must listen and be

ready to be persuaded, if necessary. Otherwise the openness of the discussion is bogus. Since the discussion is open and two-way, managers must be prepared for disagreements. Sometimes these differences may not be resolved. At least they will have seen the light of day, which must surely be much better than if they remained hidden. Each should fully understand and perhaps appreciate how the other feels. In the end, managers have the final decision on what should be done. Appraised employees may not always like what managers have decided to do, but whatever else happens, they should not be able to say that they were not given a fair hearing.

AIDE-MEMOIRE FOR A PERFORMANCE-APPRAISAL DISCUSSION

1. Meet member of staff to be appraised in advance of discussion and:
   (a) explain purpose, i.e. joint discussion of the job to analyse past performance and future needs and to decide *ACTION**
   (b) explain agenda:
       (i) the job itself (description, objectives, conditions, etc.)
       (ii) performance of component tasks
       (iii) summary of strengths and weaknesses
       (iv) future needs (training and work experience)
       (v) any other points
   (c) Agree time and place for discussion

2. Ask member of staff to:
   (a) prepare items on agenda
   (b) make self-assessment of performance and needs.

3. Carry out a joint discussion at the appointed time and place, following the broad lines of the agenda.

4. Use problem-solving, counselling techniques, i.e.:
   (a) get member of staff to give views first, to assess self, to provide possible solutions to problems
   (b) use adult – adult rather than parent – child approach
   (c) relate discussion of strengths and weaknesses of performance to actual examples (i.e. go through component tasks one by one).

5. End discussion by:
   (a) asking if member of staff is satisfied that all points have been covered.
   (b) summarizing main points of discussion.
   (c) summarizing *ACTION* to be taken by manager and member of staff.

6. Produce short written summary and pass copy to member of staff for agreement or amendment.

*POSSIBLE ACTION

Revision of:	objectives
	job description
	work methods
	resources etc.
Training:	locally – arranged by manager
	within job
	formal courses
Work experience:	changes within job
	move to another job

EXAMPLE OF A PERIODIC PERFORMANCE-APPRAISAL

- The example is intended to illustrate a systematic performance-appraisal, based on defining the tasks to be performed, the evidence of performance and the conclusions that ensue.
- In this example a periodic performance-appraisal discussion is about to be held between the Director of the Training Centre, Caledonian Engineering Company, and one of the Staff Trainers.
- The Job Description and Person Specification are given at the end of Chapter 5.
- Both prepare their notes separately, covering the job itself and the performance of each task in turn.
- The main details of the job-holder's background are these:
- Age 35.
- Employed by the company for ten years as a manager in personnel and administrative posts.
- Has degree in psychology-sociology from Open University and Diploma in Management Studies.
- Appointed to Training Centre nine months ago. No previous experience in training work.
- Attended two-week basic training-of-trainers course held at the Training Centre, given to all newly appointed trainers with no previous experience.

JOB-HOLDER'S APPRAISAL OF OWN JOB AND PERFORMANCE

The Job

- Course support staff serve several trainers at the same time. This causes regular problems about priorities and conflicts amongst trainers.
- There is a shortage of syndicate rooms for group exercises. This is a further cause of conflict amongst trainers.

Conclusions

A meeting is urgently required to be chaired by the Director and attended by all trainers. The purpose should be to discuss all possible options and to produce the best solutions.

APPRAISAL OF PERFORMANCE

	Task	Evidence	Conclusions
1.	Design and provision of cost-effective courses to meet needs of managers and staff.	Reports by trainees show general satisfaction. Some say there is too much theory and insufficient relevance to real work.	Need to discuss question of relevance with managers. Otherwise task appears to be satisfactorily performed.
2.	Selection and appointment of part-time trainers.	Present part-time trainers were inherited from predecessor. Apart from two mentioned below, evidence of performance indicates no problems.	Apart from two trainers mentioned below, no action seems to be needed.
3.	Monitoring performance of part-time trainers.	Course reports indicate satisfaction, except for Mr A and B who tend to receive below-average ratings.	Need to consider replacing Mr A and B. Otherwise part-time trainers seem to be performing well.
4.	Managing support staff.	No problems in managing support staff allocated to courses. Since they vary from course to course there is a problem with their overall management.	Support staff are managed by various trainers. They need to have one identifiable line-manager.
5.	Managing finances and material resources cost-effectively.	No major problems.	Task is being satisfactorily performed.
6.	Contributing to courses as course-leader and tutor-speaker.	Reports by trainees are favourable.	Task is being satisfactorily performed, but I would benefit from a course in the use of new technology (e.g. interactive video, Visual Reality, computer-based training).

JOB-HOLDER'S SUMMARY OF EVIDENCE AND CONCLUSIONS

As a relative newcomer to training work I think I have performed quite well in this my first year. My previous experience as a manager has been invaluable. The reports from trainees indicate that I perform well in the classroom. I have no problems in managing the support staff. I probably need to liaise closer with managers in planning courses and assessing their effectiveness. I also need to deal with the problem of inefficient part-time tutors.

Specific action to be taken

1. Meeting is needed to discuss and resolve problems of allocation of support staff and syndicate rooms.
2. Attend training course in new technology in training.

MANAGER'S APPRAISAL OF JOB-HOLDER'S JOB AND PERFORMANCE

The Job

1. In view of impending introduction of Open/Distance Learning methods into the company's training scheme the Job Description needs to include an additional task, i.e. 'Preparation of materials for Open/Distance Learning and supervision of cost-effective use'.
2. Task 2 – 'Selection and appointment of part-time trainers' – should be amended to include 'briefing part-time tutors-speakers before courses on aim, objectives, contents and methods of courses'.

Conclusions

The job-holder needs to be given further training in the use of Open and Distance learning methods.

APPRAISAL OF PERFORMANCE

	Task	Evidence	Conclusions
1.	Design and provision of cost-effective courses to meet needs of managers and staffs.	Reports by trainees and comments by managers at conference indicate excess of theory in course contents, and methods that are not job-related.	Complaint of excessive theory is an indication that the whole system needs revision, i.e. job-holder needs to consult more with managers before courses to ensure that courses meet their needs, and afterwards to ensure that training has achieved desired results. Job-holder should visit and discuss and not rely wholly on correspondence.
2.	Selection and appointment of part-time trainers.	Reports by trainees and my own personal observation indicate general satisfaction with exception of Mr A and B.	Mr A and B must be replaced. Job-holder should avoid appointment of external academics on the whole, and prefer company's own managers with a good track records. Personnel Division will help to identify suitable part-time trainers. I need personally to vet appointments in future. Job-holder should hold briefing meetings with part-time trainers before courses to explain exactly what is required. They must not be given *carte blanche* to do what they think best.
3.	Monitoring performance of part-time trainers.	Adverse comments by trainees and managers on excessive theory and deficiencies of Mr A and B.	Job-holder needs to get a tighter grip. He must sit-in more during courses and observe for himself.
4.	Managing support staff.	Own observations and discussions with support staff indicate satisfaction.	Job-holder is strong in interpersonal relationships and manages support staff well.
5.	Managing finances and material resources cost-effectively.	Own checks and observations indicate sound management in general.	Job-holder performs this task satisfactorily. Before purchasing training films, he needs to pre-view to confirm usefulness.
6.	Contributing to courses as course-leader and tutor-speaker.	Own observations and reports by course members indicate satisfactory performance.	In the classroom the job-holder is a very competent performer. He plans his material well and is a skilful presenter and tutor.

MANAGER'S SUMMARY

General Summary of Evidence and Conclusions

The job-holder has a pleasant and co-operative demeanour. He approaches work with interest and enthusiasm and is ever willing to learn. He relates well with colleagues of all levels and with trainees and their managers. This is his first training job in which he is still developing. In the classroom he performs effectively. His lack of experience is much more evident behind the scenes. He needs to improve and develop skills in the management of training, i.e. identifying needs, designing and providing needs-related, realistic training programmes, assessing training effectiveness. At this stage he cannot be assessed as fully achieving the purpose of the job. However, he should be capable of satisfying the required standards with further experience, development and training.

Specific Action to be Taken

By Job-holder

1. Involve managers in training system as follows:
   (a) Use questionnaires and visits to ascertain what their staffs need to learn.
   (b) Get their approval of proposed aim, objectives, contents and methods before courses are actually conducted.
   (c) After courses, use questionnaires and visits to ascertain views of managers and ex-trainees on actual effectiveness of training in job-related terms and on any proposals for change.

2. (a) Replace Mr A and B as tutor-speakers.
   (b) Consult with Personnel Division to identify operational managers and supervisors with potential to perform effectively as part-time tutor-speakers.
   (c) Hold briefing meetings before courses to ensure that part-time staff fully understand what they are required to do and how their contributions serve the course aim and objectives.

3. (a) Sit in regularly when courses are in progress to assess performance of part-time tutors.
   (b) Give them feedback on performance and discuss.

4. Before purchasing training films, confirm their usefulness by pre-viewing and hiring for short term.

By Manager

1. Hold meeting with all training officers to resolve problems with:
   (a) management of support staff;
   (b) allocation of support staff;
   (c) allocation of syndicate rooms.

2. Arrange developmental training programme for job-holder to cover:
   (a) management of training;
   (b) Open and Distance Learning methods;
   (c) use of new technology in training.

3. Personally vet appointment of part-time tutor-speakers.

Notes

1. The example summary by the manager assumes that the manager's conclusions, made before discussion with the job-holder were confirmed. In practice, some of the manager's original views could be modified by what the job-holder has to say.
2. The summary will be discussed and agreed with the job-holder, who receives a copy for retention and action.
3. It is most important that agreed action is actually carried out. This is discussed at the next regular performance-appraisal discussion, for example, in three months' time.

EXERCISE ON PERFORMANCE-APPRAISAL

- Choose a member of your work-group to try out the appraisal methods illustrated in the example at the end of this chapter.
- Define the purpose of the job.
- List the tasks that must be effectively performed to achieve the purpose of the job.
- Using the format shown in the example, get the job-holder to assess him or herself.
- Carry out your own assessment in the same way.
- Discuss and compare assessments and produce conclusions and proposed actions.

CHAPTER 9

Developing Abilities and Improving Performance

BASIC QUESTIONS

1 Why is so much importance now given to developing and improving the abilities of employees?
2 In what ways may managers develop and improve the abilities of employees at the work-place?
3 How should training be defined in terms of the process and purpose?
4 What is meant by cost-effective training?
5 What are the main stages and requirements of a cost-effective system?
6 What role should managers play in implementing a cost-effective training system?

Questioned about the manager's role, Sir John Harvey-Jones, formerly chairman of ICI and now a well-known consultant and commentator on management, recently said that helping people to develop their abilities and to improve their performance is one of a manager's major roles. In former times when managerial styles were predominantly authoritarian and managers were mainly task-oriented, this role was rarely recognized or put into effective practice. The manager's principal role, it was thought, was to see that required work was carried out satisfactorily and on time. The idea that managers should give the development of staff a high priority and devote considerable time and resources to this end would probably have been seen as an unnecessary and expensive luxury.

Considerable research into people at work, the effects of organizational culture and management styles on productivity and motivation, have demonstrated the short-sightedness and error of this view. Investment in developing an organization's human resources pays significant dividends. It is a major factor in improving the performance of individuals, groups and organizations. At the same time, it should create a more competent, versatile, contented, motivated work-force, committed to achieving organizational goals and less likely to waste time in conflict and negative behaviour. Not only have managerial attitudes changed with the passage of time, but so also have employees' expectations. Opportunities for personal development are commonly regarded as an important part of the employment contract. The fundamental changes in attitudes and practice *vis-à-vis* the development of employees have become increasingly evident in recent times. Politicians and union leaders regularly emphasize the crucial importance of training for purposes of industrial competence and economic growth. Human resources development – a term of comparatively recent origin – receives considerable attention in literature and training courses concerned with management. Some universities now have departments and academic staff concerned solely with the subject. Continuous change in technology and in work-practices in recent times has been a very significant factor in focusing attention on the importance of human resources development.

The main responsibility for policy and effective practice is a matter for the senior management. However, it is the junior managers who are in the front line. They are in daily contact with work-groups and are directly and continually responsible for supervising the development of the members of their teams. In the end it is they who make the decisions about who needs help of this kind and in what form.

Textbooks concerned with management, personnel management and related themes regularly attempt to define and distinguish terms such as training, development and education. Ask specialists in the field to differentiate between training and development and different answers may be provided. In practice, the lines between training and development are often blurred. It probably makes linguistic and logical sense to regard the development of human resources as the total process and training as a major element. Anyway, the terms are relatively unimportant. What really matters is that managers should give a very high priority to developing abilities and improving the performance of people for whose work they are responsible. Managerial style is obviously of crucial importance for the achievement of these purposes. By allotting time regularly to each individual to discuss work, its performance, problems, possible solutions and proposed action for help, managers are able to ensure that individual needs for development and improvement of performance are kept under constant review and receive the necessary attention.

The democratic-participative style enables managers to acquire the necessary information as a basis for decisions to meet the developmental needs of the members of their work-groups. It is also quite likely and possible that the very practice of the style itself may have a developmental influence and effect on individuals in a subtle and imperceptible way. People learn by example and imitation. Without realizing it, individual members of the work-group might well be beneficially influenced by constant exposure to the effects of a democratic-participative style of management. One obvious possible effect could be the development of positive attitudes. Having the requisite knowledge and skills is not enough for effective performance of work. They must be accompanied by appropriate attitudes, such as enthusiasm, commitment, conscientious-ness, co-operativeness, etc. These are hardly likely to be developed by training courses in the same way that knowledge and skills may be. The behaviour of managers is, therefore, very important as an example for others to copy.

Abilities may be developed and performance improved in a variety of ways. Two broad categories of methods may be identified, which provide appropriate headings for a detailed analysis of methods and possible benefits, i.e. work experience and training.

DEVELOPING PEOPLE BY WORK EXPERIENCE

Normally, people learn and develop abilities by themselves from the sheer exposure to the varying situations and contingencies of real work itself. Over time they will learn that one way is better than another to perform certain tasks. They will learn from observing work-colleagues. They will learn from mistakes which hopefully will help them to avoid similar errors in the future. Training is fundamentally important in pointing trainees in the right direction and providing them with the basis for effective performance in the future, but in the end the experience of work itself is the best teacher.

Managers who approach their developmental role conscientiously will always be on the look-out for opportunities to structure the learning experience that actual work itself can provide. Some of these have already been mentioned as methods that could be included in an induction programme to help newly appointed employees to settle, e.g. working under the tutelage of experienced colleagues ('sitting by Nelly'), coaching, job-rotation, visits and attachments. All of these methods can be used at any time for developmental purposes. In addition to these methods there are two others, described below, that are potentially very fruitful for the purposes of developing people through work experience.

The first of these methods is the use of events of normal work, that require effective organization and planning over a period of time, for developmental purposes. Such events could be, for example, an exhibition, a conference or social activity. The possibilities are numerous. There is no specific term to describe the method. It might be described perhaps as a delegated project or assignment. A particular advantage of the method is that it may be given to one employee or to several as a small group. The manager structures the task in the following way:

1. A thorough briefing is given to those who are to carry out these tasks, covering the aim, standards expected, resources available – people, money, equipment, time-scale – etc.
2. They are then required to produce a detailed plan for the task by an agreed date.
3. The plan is discussed in detail with managers and amended as might be necessary.
4. The employees concerned then put the plan into action and make all the preparations necessary to ensure that the event is successful.
5. Managers make periodic checks to see that all is going smoothly. The employees concerned may refer to managers at any time they feel they need advice and help.
6. There is a final meeting before the event itself to ensure that everything is ready and that nothing has been overlooked.
7. When the event is over there is a final meeting to evaluate the learning achievement and developmental benefits. The main questions are obviously: How successfully was the project-assignment accomplished? What did the employees who undertook the tasks learn from the experience? Throughout the planning of the tasks the manager's behaviour is very important for the achievement of its developmental purposes. The role is not altogether unlike that of a driving instructor. The pupil has to be allowed to carry out the task without excessive interference or prescription. Otherwise the whole purpose of the exercise may well be negated. At the same time, the event itself has to

be successfully planned and implemented. Managers still carry the can if it turns out badly: They cannot pass it off by saying that it was only a training exercise. The particular advantages of this developmental method are these:

(a) They are usually multifaceted, involving planning, organizing, using a variety of resources, corresponding with people by spoken and written word.

(b) Being based on real events at work, the learning potential is considerable.

(c) They may shed light on potential as yet not revealed.

(d) They are especially helpful means of developing initiative, self-reliance and confidence.

(e) Since it is possible to involve several employees in the same task, there is an additional possible benefit in the development of effective teamwork. There may well be all kinds of tasks that could be used for developmental purposes in this way. Again, it all depends on managers' attitudes and behaviour. They need to be trusting, not frightened to delegate, adventurous and imaginative in their use of opportunities.

The second method that can be used with considerable effect for employee-development is involvement of the work-group in problem-solving and decision-making. This is a major function of the manager's job. If they are autocratic in style, they will solve problems and take decisions in solitary isolation. If they are disposed towards the democratic-participative style and do not believe that they have all the answers, they will involve the members of their groups and get the benefit of a diversity of opinions. To achieve this purpose the work-group needs to meet regularly for discussions. These are meetings with a purpose and not the kind of fixed weekly or monthly meetings, which can be a potential source of much wasted time and frustration. They are held at the manager's discretion, whenever necessary and at the convenience of group-members. They are a means whereby the group-members exchange and share information, ask each other questions in an open, frank atmosphere. Managers chair the meetings with a *primus inter pares* approach. They are not there to dominate and dictate, but to ensure that everyone has a chance to contribute and that in the end the best solutions are found. How can meetings of this kind further the cause of employee development? They encourage individuals to say what they truly feel. At the same time, they help people to develop skills in asking and listening, to appreciate that others may have views different from their own, which must be respected with tolerance. They help to develop skills in clear, logical thinking for the analysis of problems. Finally, they should help to foster cooperation and team spirit.

How does the development of people through work experience differ from developing them by means of training? There are two main differences. The use of work experience as a means of enhancing performance is undoubtedly worthwhile, valuable and necessary. However, it has to be said that it is a somewhat imprecise method in terms of the measurement of learning achievement. Learning in this way is a subtle process. The effects may take some time to make themselves seen. Managers may involve employees in problem-solving, decision-making projects, etc., confident that a number of benefits should ensue to improve future performance of work. Nevertheless, these effects cannot usually be seen in the same way that, say, the results of a training course in typing would be evident. When training courses are given, it is important – in most cases at least – to be able to measure as precisely as possible the effects on the performance of work not too long after the completion of training. Thus, training is designed to achieve specific, work-related results.

The second difference concerns costs. There are little or no costs incurred when work experience is used as a means of employee-development. Here, tasks which had to be carried out anyway are used as media for developmental purposes. Employees under training, on the other hand, are not normally productive whilst training is in progress. There are costs to be met, and this makes cost-effectiveness an issue of primary importance when training is used to develop employees' abilities and to improve their performance.

DEVELOPING PEOPLE BY TRAINING

What is training? It is a process initiated by employers who invest resources with the purpose of helping employees to learn and practise specific knowledge, skills and attitudes identified as necessary for the effective performance of work. A wide range of methods is available to achieve the purposes of training. The sole criterion determining choice should be cost-effectiveness, i.e. which methods are most likely most economically to achieve the required results.

A comprehensive definition of this kind is important because it leads to a number of logical consequences that are the bases of effective practice.

1. When all is said and done, the ultimate question is: Has training had its intended effect on subsequent work and performance? If it has failed to do so, then it has probably incurred a considerable waste of time and money. This is a vitally important consideration. Recent surveys of training effectiveness in major organizations have revealed disturbing examples of people being sent on training courses that they did not really need or that did not meet their work-needs.
2. To ensure that training is as cost-effective as it can possibly be, a logical sequence of questions need to be asked and answered, i.e.:
    (a) Have the requirements for effective performance been properly defined? If not, it is manifestly pointless to provide training to meet ill-defined criteria.
    (b) Is performance regularly appraised? If not, there is no systematic means of identifying needs.
    (c) If performance-appraisal has revealed any gaps between actual performance and what is required for effectiveness, is training the right solution?
    (d) If the answer is 'yes' to the first three questions, precisely who needs training and what do they need to learn?
    (e) What should the aim and objectives of training be in order to achieve the required learning?
    (f) Which forms and methods of training are likely to be the most cost-effective in meeting employees' needs?
    (g) At the end of training have the defined aim and objectives been achieved?
    (h) After a lapse of time does an appraisal of performance indicate that training has achieved its intended purposes?
    (i) If not, where do the faults lie and what changes need to be made?
3. Managers are responsible for effective performance of work. They are, therefore, responsible for taking all the major decisions that arise from the questions listed above. The role of trainers is subordinate. Their task is to meet managers' requirements and to provide any specialist advice and assistance they may need.

As questions 2 (a) (b) and (c) indicate, the training system must be based on a definition of the requirements for effective performance, the criteria, and on an appraisal of actual performance of work as the evidence on which judgements are based.

Questions 2 (d)–(i) are commonly described as a Systems Approach to Training (SAT). They are a series of logically sequential, interdependent stages designed to ensure that the right training is given to the right people, at the right time, in the right form. It is a rigorous discipline, but the only possible route to the achievement of cost-effectiveness in training.

The requirements of this disciplined approach should leave no doubt about the extent and importance of the role of managers in training. They must play a leading part at every stage of the system from start to finish. As well as managing the training system, they may be required from time to time to fulfil an instructional role, certainly at the work-place and sometimes at organizational training centres as occasional contributors to training courses. They need, therefore, to have knowledge of and skills in training design and provision that are substantially the same as training specialists. They also need the speaking skills, described in detail in Chapter 3 (2). The specialist nature of training has tended to be overrated. In truth, the requirements for effectiveness as a trainer differ little from the requirements for effective management in terms of organizing, planning, interpersonal skills of asking, listening, speaking to groups and leading groups in discussions. Managers may not be so well versed in the techniques and methods of training as full-time trainers, but these can soon be learned.

MANAGING THE TRAINING SYSTEM

STAGE I   Identification of Needs

Apart from training which may be mandatory for certain groups of employees, e.g. new recruits, managers, personnel managers, trainers, etc., the responsibility for identifying developmental and training needs rests with individual managers. The occasions when needs are confirmed and the necessary action is decided are induction interviews and performance-appraisal discussions. Whilst managers must take the final decisions on whether needs exist and what the appropriate action should be to meet any identified needs, the individuals concerned also need to be involved in the decisions. The use of induction interviews and performance-appraisal discussions for purposes of assessing needs has already been discussed in the chapters covering these subjects.

The most important points that should be emphasized are these:

1. **Needs may arise at any time**. This is one of the reasons why managers should hold regular performance-appraisal discussions with the individual members of their staffs. It is not a matter that can be left to an annual review.
2. **It must involve individual members of staff**. They ought to learn to assess themselves and to become aware of their own needs. At the same time, discussions of this kind with their managers should encourage them to analyse their own performance and to find solutions for their own needs and problems.

STAGE 2   Design and Provision of Needs-related Training

Whether they realize it or not managers have a leading role in the design and provision of needs-related training. To achieve the cost-effective purposes of training, managers and trainers need to plan training along the following lines:

1. To take account of factors that affect learning.
2. To define the aim and objectives, i.e. the required learning-achievement.
3. To plan training to meet the defined aim and objectives, taking account of contents (subjects to be learned), the most appropriate forms and methods for learning and means of assessing learning achievement.

The Learning Process

Developing the abilities of employees at work is essentially a learning process. Galileo, the 15-16th-century Italian scientist, is supposed to have made the wise comment: 'You cannot teach anyone anything. You can only help them to learn', i.e. the trainer's role is essentially one of helping and motivating.

The subject of human learning has been discussed and debated in the textbooks on psychology for many years, sometimes with controversy. These recondite issues need not concern people who may be involved in developing the organization's human resources. What they need to know in simple terms is – what is learning, and what do common sense and experience show about how people may be helped most effectively to learn what they need. Learning may be described as a change in a person's knowledge, skills, attitudes and personal attributes, brought about by external influences. The external influences that affect human learning are often casual and unplanned. We are all subjected to them continually from the first to the last breath. Young people are not taught to smoke. They learn the habit because they see others doing it and decide that it is a smart thing to do. The current debate about crime and violence is concerned with whether people learn this behaviour from television and films. When learning takes place in the context of education and training, the learning influences are structured and controlled.

Whether learning is casual or planned, there always needs to be a demonstration to indicate that a change has taken place. Carrying an umbrella is an indication that people have learned that rain makes them wet. Pupils may solemnly assure their teachers that they have studied hard and learned what they had to learn. Nevertheless, they still have to take examinations to show what they have learned. Current arguments about educational testing are all about the demonstration of learning achievement.

So much for what learning is. The questions that those who design and provide learning opportunities for people at work have to consider are – how do people learn and how does this affect methods to be used? There is a broad consensus that the following factors are of primary importance.

Motivation. Learning depends on motivation. People need to be able to see the benefit and relevance of the learning that has been planned for them, i.e. what is its relevance? How will it help them to perform their jobs more effectively? How could it satisfy their personal needs, e.g. for growth, achievement, etc?

The basic importance of the motivational factor in learning can be seen all the time in the education of children. Because of their inevitable immaturity, it is often extremely difficult to persuade them to see any point in learning. Some see no point in it at all. They are not motivated nor stimulated to pay attention, and in consequences rebel and absent themselves.

Feedback. This is linked to the motivational factor. People need to know how they are progressing, what they have achieved, what they still need to learn.

Individual differences and their effects on the learning process. It is no doubt important to be aware of these in general terms when learning opportunities are being planned. At the same time, managers, trainers and others involved in the task can hardly be expected to identify the idiosyncrasies of each individual learner and to produce custom-built learning material on this basis. The most important difference that needs to be taken into account is the variation in rates of learning. This is caused by factors such as differences in aptitudes, mental characteristics, interests and age. Some people absorb foreign languages more easily than others; some find mathematics difficult; others do not. Older people may not learn in the same ways or with the same facility and speed as they did when they were younger. These differences have an important bearing on the choice of the most appropriate learning methods.

Example and imitation. The effects of these factors in the learning process have already been mentioned when the nature of learning was being considered. People are influenced by them all the time. They are powerful forces that can change behaviour for the worse as well as for the better.

The senses. All five senses may be used as channels by which learning occurs. Of these, obviously the eyes and ears are the most important.

We can now consider how these basic factors may affect the planning and provision of learning opportunities. Those who have to undertake these tasks need to:

- start with relevance and motivation in the forefront of their thinking. They need to ask themselves: What do people need to learn and why? What is the relevance to the effective performance of work? Which methods are likely to be the most effective in achieving the purposes of learning?;
- be aware of the fundamental importance of motivation to learn. They should discuss these questions at the very outset with learners to help them to see that the proposed learning has important benefits for them.
- be flexible in the use of a variety of methods in order to take account of individual differences in the learning process and at the same time to stimulate interest;
- use methods that are directly relevant to the actual situations and needs of work. For example, it sometimes happens that people attending training courses are given exercises which may be enjoyable but are very doubtful value in terms of learning what is really needed for the effective performance of work;
- use methods that are active and participative. Such methods are likely to be more interesting than passive methods, but, most important of all, they enable learning to be demonstrated.

Defining Aims and Objectives of Training

A clear definition of aims and objectives is essential to cost-effective training for the following reasons:

1. They specify what learning trainees are expected to achieve by the end of their training.
2. They indicate what the contents and methods ought to be in order to achieve the defined aims and objectives.
3. They are the criteria for assessing whether training has achieved its purposes or not.

The aim is a general statement of the overall achievement that is required. Objectives specify the various subsidiary requirements to achieve the aim. Care and skill is needed in writing them. Well-defined objectives should:

- specify what learning trainees should be able to demonstrate by the end of training;
- be expressed in learner-orientated terms. A standard formula for writing training objectives is to begin with the words: 'By the end of training trainees should be able to . . . ;
- be expressed in action language, e.g.
  (a) 'Trainees should be able to define the requirements for effective management.'
  (b) 'Trainees should be able to conduct an effective selection interview (in accordance with the defined criteria for effectiveness).' The words 'define' and 'conduct' emphasize that learning has to be demonstrated and logically affect the contents and methods of the course;
- be realistic and achievable, i.e. in the time available. For example, if a trainer is allocated three days for a course on skills in public speaking for people with no previous experience, what could realistically be achieved in that time? Achievement would naturally vary from one trainee to another, depending on individual aptitudes and learning capacity. In general, however, a three-day course would be very limited in its potential achievement. Trainees should at least be able to define the requirements for effective performance in public speaking. They also ought to be able to demonstrate in practice that they have learned a basis of the essential skills to be developed after the course through further practice and experience. The realistic aim of a course such as this should be to point trainees in the right direction and to send them away

with sound foundations for future personal development. The contents and methods would then be designed to achieve this purpose;

- be as measurable as possible. The possibility of accurate measurement of learning-achievement varies considerably in accordance with the nature of the subject. In training soldiers to fire weapons, it is easy to assess whether they are adopting the correct posture and how many times they hit or miss the target. When subjects are much more complicated, such as management, for example, or related subjects, the assessment of learning achievement is often much more difficult. This is not a reason for abandoning the task. Managers and trainers have to do the best they can and accept that total accuracy is not always possible;
- specify as precisely as possible the required performance, standards and conditions of required performance at the end of training.

Here is a simple example of the aim and objectives for a course for trainee-typists.

AIM

By the end of training, trainee-typists should be able to perform effectively all the typing tasks required by the employing organization.

OBJECTIVES

By the end of training, trainee-typists should be able to type all forms of correspondence and documents used in actual work:

(a) using formats specified by the employing organization;
(b) to a specific level of accuracy (e.g. 100%);
(c) at a specific rate (e.g. x words per minute);
(d) using copy, audio and word-processor methods.

Aims and objectives expressed in this form are required for an entire programme, but also for each individual subject contained in the programme. In introducing a course or a single subject, the first thing that trainers and tutors must do is tell the trainees what the aims and objectives are, so that they know from the outset what they need to learn and what standards they are expected to achieve.

CHOOSING THE MOST COST-EFFECTIVE FORMS AND METHODS

There are essentially three forms that training may take. They can be differentiated in terms of locations and training providers, i.e. at the work-place, at training centres, internal or external, a combination of the methods of the work-place and training centres. To make the right choices managers need to carry out a cost-benefit analysis, based on a knowledge of the methods available and the potential value of each as learning media. Nowadays because of emphasis that has been given to training, most managers are familiar with the commonly used forms and methods. What factors do they need to take into account when making choices? Before this question is considered, it ought to be emphasized that this is not primarily a matter of deciding that one form or method is better than another. Rather, it is a question of deciding which is the most cost-effective to meet the needs of particular situations.

At the Work-place

1. When people are trained at the work-place, training is naturally directed towards the needs of work. There is very little possibility of training being provided that is either unnecessary or irrelevant.
2. Managers or their deputies are in direct control of training and should, therefore, be able to ensure that it achieves its aim and objectives.
3. Learning achievement can be immediately assessed in terms of work performance, and any deficiencies be quickly remedied.
4. Work colleagues who are both experienced and competent are available to assist managers in the design and provision of needs-related training.
5. Training can be flexibly arranged to take account of the demands of work. At the same time, if managers do not give a high priority to their training role or are excessively task-orientated, training may be neglected. It may be regularly postponed, cancelled or interrupted because of what managers perceive as urgent work that must be attended to immediately.
6. Being experienced and competent in performing jobs is one thing; having the required knowledge and skills effectively to train other people is another. It is very important, therefore, that managers and their deputies who design and provide training should attend short

training courses in these subjects to furnish them with sound bases for these tasks.

7. The costs of training people at the work-place are obviously very considerably less than sending people to attend off-job training centres.

At Training Centres

Training centres exist to provide training for groups of people with shared needs – new recruits, managers, personnel and training staff, etc. Centres may be permanent establishments within or outside the employing organizations, or they may be temporary centres, such as hotels in the countryside or by the sea.

Factors to be considered in assessing the potential value of this form of training are these:

1. People from various parts of an organization or from different organizations with common work interests and experience, can meet, learn together and from each other, share experience, discuss and solve common problems. Quite apart from any knowledge or skills that the course itself may impart, the opportunity for communication with other people employed in similar work can be a by-product of inestimable value.
2. Away from the pressures and problems of work, trainees can stand back, take a detached view of themselves, gain valuable insight into how others see them, and have an opportunity for some uncluttered thinking.
3. Away from their places of work they can learn from their mistakes during the active-learning parts of training that could be serious, costly or personally embarrassing, if they were made at the work-place.
4. Training centres can offer not only expertise from full-time training staff, but also from a range of external speakers and specialists, whom trainees would otherwise not have an opportunity of meeting.
5. Training centres can provide possibilities of the use of a wide range of activities, methods and aids to learning.
6. Training centres are very costly in terms of accommodation, equipment and staff.
7. They are also costly in trainee terms. Trainees have to travel sometimes long distances and to be given board and lodging. There is also what

economists would describe as the opportunity costs of trainees' absence from productive employment at the work-site.

8. Women who have responsibilities for children and homes may sometimes find difficulties in attending training centres.

9. If managers have not been consulted about training design – and this is inevitable with external training – there is always the possibility that training may not be relevant to the needs of work.

As always, cost-effectiveness is the principal criterion in choosing forms and methods of training, i.e. they must be seen to meet the real requirements of work. It follows logically, therefore, that managers must be closely involved in the design of training at training centres that are part of the employing organization. To set up costly training centres and leave the training staff to provide any training in whatever way they think best is a very serious dereliction of responsibility on the part of management, and certain to ensure that training is not cost-effective.

Any course provided by an organizational training centre must be the result of identified work-needs and dialogue between managers and trainers about aim, objectives and contents. Training methods are a matter for trainers to decide, but managers must still be involved in the design to ensure that training meets real requirements of work. This communication between managers and trainers does not happen by chance. It has to be standard practice and achieved by means of meetings, discussions, questionnaires, etc.

When training is provided by external training institutes, managers obviously cannot be involved in this way in the design of training. They need, therefore, to study very carefully what the training institute says about its courses in terms of aims, objectives, contents, methods, staff for whom training is intended. If this information is not clearly defined, especially in terms of expected learning achievement, there is cause for suspicion. Any employees sent on external courses must produce a comprehensive report for their employers, assessing the suitability of learning methods, what they have learned and how it might help their work performance. Two or three reports of this kind can help managers decide whether it is worthwhile sending other employees for external training.

Training designers must always have the notion of relevance to work in the forefront of their thinking, when choosing appropriate methods for learning. The question of relevance is more of a possible problem when training is provided at centres than it is with work-place training. If managers do not liaise closely with training staffs, there is a danger that contents and methods may not meet the real needs of work. As a very general rule, the closer training-methods are to the realities of work the better. This is why methods such as case-studies, based on real events at work, simulation and role play, are especially useful as learning media. The particular advantages of participative methods are these:

1. They can be designed to create learning experiences that are directly transferable to work.
2. They involve all trainees in the learning experience, whether as direct participants or observers.
3. As the methods are work-related, trainees can see their relevance and benefits and become, therefore, motivated and stimulated.
4. They enable learning-achievement to be assessed, because the activity requires knowledge and skills to be demonstrated.
5. They can be recorded on CCTV, which is a very powerful medium for learning, allowing trainees to study and critically examine their own performance and behaviour.

Whilst training staff have a general responsibility for the methods used on courses, it is important that managers should have a good knowledge of methods available, their potential benefits as means of relevant learning, and trainer-skills in using them. First, this knowledge is useful and necessary when discussing the value and relevance of recent training with the members of their staffs. Secondly, managers may well be required from time to time to contribute to courses at training centres as speakers or tutors.

Combining Methods of Work-place and Centres

The pressure for cost-effectiveness, coupled with technological advances, have opened up new vistas for training in recent years. In former times the need for training frequently required employers to leave the work-place to attend courses at centres. Nowadays it has become increasingly obvious that cost-effectiveness requires more flexibility in training and that flexible methods have proven their potential for effective learning. The pros and cons of training at centres have already been discussed. Two particular disadvantages mentioned were costs and the need for people to leave their work-places. The experience and success achieved by the Open University over a number of years has given clear evidence of what learning can be achieved by self-study methods, always provided that the learning material is of the highest possible quality and the students have constant support and advice available. The major weakness of traditional correspondence courses was that material was not always well structured and presented, and that enormous demands were made on the perseverance, self-discipline and motivation of the students. When open or distance learning methods started to be introduced into the work-place, some scepticism was expressed at first because of the experience of the problems and weaknesses of correspondence courses. However, sufficient time has now elapsed for the cost-effectiveness of these methods to be properly assessed in the work-place. It is significant that several captains of industry with obvious vested interests in the cost-effectiveness of their business have strongly supported open and distance methods of training. Because some people get carried away with excessive enthusiasm for these methods, it needs to be repeated that various methods are suited to particular situations. Open and distance methods do not replace all other methods. They have considerable advantages, but there is still a need for certain forms of training to take place in groups at training centres for reasons already explained.

Material is produced by training staff. It may include textbooks, video films, audio-tapes, computer programs or inter-active video. Like any other form of training, it is based on work-needs of employees, providing them with audio-visual presentations of subjects to be learned. Because motivation is so important in learning, and especially when it is presented in this form, the material must be as attractive and stimulating as it can possibly be. It is a progressive, structured learning process in which trainees are required to answer questions and to solve problems as a demonstration of learning-achievement. Just as with courses at training centres it is essential that managers be consulted and involved at all stages of production. The production and distribution of this material throughout all the sites and offices is costly. Therefore, before it is mass-produced, two preparatory measures are essential. First, the learning package needs to be finally checked for accuracy and potential effectiveness with the operational staff who are professionally qualified in the subject in question. Secondly, it needs to be tried and tested by means of a pilot scheme to ascertain in practice whether it really achieves the learning purposes as intended.

The problems of motivation, concentration, self-discipline and the effects of isolation that have limited the effectiveness of traditional correspondence courses need to be remembered and avoided. Because study takes place mainly at the work-place, much depends on the support, advice and supervision that managers provide. The particular requirements for the effective use of these methods are:

1. Managers should prepare a timetable for regular study, which should only be changed because of extreme pressure of work.
2. They should provide a study room to house learning material and equipment so that trainees can work in comfort and quiet.
3. They should have regular discussions with trainees to monitor progress. Alternatively, they should appoint a responsible competent deputy to supervise trainees' studies.
4. The central training staff should be in regular contact with trainees and their managers and make periodic visits to trainees' places of work for discussions and feedback and to see whether material needs any revision.

Benefits of Open and Distance Methods

Those with significant experience of the methods confirm and report the following benefits:

1. Compared with similar courses at training centres, they are more cost-effective. Despite the cost of producing a large number of learning packages and installing video and computer equipment at numerous sites throughout the organization, these costs are almost always significantly less than the total costs of courses held at training centres.
2. They are especially suitable for vocational and clerical types of work, where learning in groups is not an important part of the learning process.
3. The methods are extremely flexible. Study can take place at any time and at any place. Training can be adapted to suit schedules and pressures of work.
4. Training can be related and applied to actual work immediately.
5. The methods take full account of the different paces at which individuals learn. Fast learners are not delayed. Slow learners are not rushed or left behind.
6. Material can be repeated over and over again, as the trainee wishes.
7. The individual's learning achievement is being continuously and progressively tested.
8. The material could be used by other members of staff to update knowledge and skills.

9. Properly produced and supervised there are no significant disadvantages in the methods.

Serial Short Courses

Some subjects, such as management are much too complicated to encompass satisfactorily in one short course. For example, newly appointed managers are often sent away for courses lasting for two or three weeks at the most. Inevitably, the various subjects of management that one might expect to find on the contents page of a textbook receive very superficial treatment. Small wonder that ex-trainees, when retrospectively assessing the effectiveness of their training, conclude that it did little of significance to help them with their real work. The problem is made even worse if these two- or three-week courses contain a considerable quantity of textbook theory, as they often do. Obviously, what is needed is longer courses to do each subject justice, with much more emphasis on the practical realities of the job. If training continues to be provided in the conventional way, it is in effect only paying lip-service to the need, and wasting a considerable amount of time, effort and money.

Several organizations have provided an answer to the problem, which experience has shown to be extremely effective.

The essential features of the serial short-course method are these:

1. The component elements of a subject are produced as a series of interdependent short courses, e.g. three days each.
2. There are intervals between each short course of several weeks, e.g. five or six.
3. In these intervals at trainees' work-places, they are required to carry out assignments in which they apply the learning of the short course to real work situations. For example, after a short course on time-management, trainees might be required to analyse how their own time is managed and how well their work-colleagues manage their time. They might also be required to read hand-out material, articles or textbooks and answer questions. The assignments carried out at the work-place are supervised by their managers or a suitable deputy.
4. Assignments are regarded as practical tests of work-related learning and are assessed by the training-centre staff.

The advantages of this method, already tried and proven, are these:

1. It combines the benefits of work-place and training-centre training.
2. It enables whatever is learned at the training centre to be applied directly to real work situations. Relevance is immediately tested.
3. The effects of training on actual work performance can be assessed immediately and progressively.
4. There is close collaboration between training-centre staff, managers and trainees.

Programmes of this kind are intended primarily for subjects where trainees are best trained in groups because of the benefits of discussions, exchanges of views, learning from others. This form of training is lengthier and more costly than traditional methods. All the same, to persist in giving people short courses for complicated subjects such as management, for example, where the treatment is superficial and the learning achievement inevitably very limited, is only paying lip-service to training needs and is a 'penny wise – pound foolish' approach.

EXAMPLE OF SERIAL SHORT-COURSE METHODS

TRAINING PROGRAMME FOR NEWLY APPOINTED MANAGERS

Course No.	Subject
1.	Management – its nature and essentials.
2.	Human behaviour – individuals, motivation, groups.
3.	Communication.
4.	Leadership.
5.	Interpersonal skills.
6.	Organization of work and management of time.
7.	Problem-solving and decision-making.
8.	Human resources development.
9.	Managing financial and material resources.
10.	Modern technology, techniques and effects on management and work.
11.	Summary of programme and assessment of learning.

Each short course would probably last from two to five days, depending on the subject.
Intervals between courses would probably be from four to six weeks.

STAGE 3   Assessing the Effectiveness of Training

Assessing the effectiveness of training requires answers to two questions:

- Have the aim and objectives been achieved?
- Has training had the required effects on the subsequent performance of work?

If the aim and objectives of the performance and the requirements for effective performance of work have not been defined or inadequately expressed, then there will be no criteria for making judgements and the questions cannot be answered. The assessment of the effectiveness of learning achievement needs to be made during training, at the end of training and after training. In basic terms, the assessment is the same whether training takes place at or away from the place of work. The main question about effects on work-performance is all that ultimately matters. Has the investment of resources, time and effort been worthwhile?

The methods of assessment are broadly the same for all forms of work-directed learning, e.g. tests, meetings, discussions, questionnaires. When any form of training occurs at the work-place, the assessment will normally be made only by managers and the members of their staffs. In these circumstances, assessment is relatively easier because training methods are usually closely related to or part of work itself. Results are more immediately observable in terms of work-performance.

When people attend courses at training centres, the training staffs must obviously be involved. However, they can only assess whether the training aim and objectives have been achieved. Only managers and their ex-trainee members of staff can comment on effects on work-performance.

Assessment During Training

Assessment is made by tests designed to measure learning achievement, and from the evidence of participative methods.

Assessment at the End of Training

Methods are similar to those used during training and include a final test of achievement, designed to ascertain whether the training aim has been achieved. When training has taken place at training centres, it is also customary to seek the views of trainees by means of questionnaires and open-forum discussions. These views are obviously important, but their value is limited. They are inevitably subjective, reflect personal opinions not always universally agreed, are affected perhaps by end-of-course euphoria, lack the perspective of time and distance, and have not been tested in work experience. The views of trainees can be considerably enhanced in value by the following means:

1. **Requiring trainees to keep learning-assessment records**. They have to make notes at the end of each day to record what they think they have learned from each subject in the programme.
2. **Providing them with a questionnaire to complete before the training ends and before any discussion is held**. Questions are concerned with the value of training to the trainees and with suggestions for any changes and improvements they consider necessary. Any criticisms made must be constructive and include examples to support views. It is not enough for trainees to say that they did not find a particular subject useful. They have to say why, and what they would recommend.

Assessment After Training

Good managers will always have discussions with members of their staffs on completion of a training programme. This is especially important when people return to work after an off-job training course. Managers need to listen to what they have to say about the value of the training and how they think it could be effectively applied to their work. The discussion has to be a structured investigation. It is not a matter of casually inquiring: 'How did you enjoy the course?' It can be very demotivating for people to return to work eager to put new learning into practice to find that their managers are only mildly interested or perhaps even not interested at all.

A further final discussion is helpful after a lapse of time to consider the ultimate question – did training achieve its purposes in terms of subsequent work-performances? Did it give value for money? This discussion demonstrates the need for and value of regular performance-appraisal discussions between managers and the individual members of their staffs. If regular, scheduled discussions are taking place about work-performance, an analysis of the benefits of any recent training is an obvious item for inclusion in the agenda.

When training is held at training centres, both managers and trainers have a vested interest in the assessment of training and its cost-effectiveness. Considering the effects on actual performance will also indicate whether any changes are needed, especially since the views of all ex-trainees and their managers can and should be sought. Managers and ex-trainees can, of course, give feedback to central trainers without prompting, whenever they wish to do so. Obtaining collective feedback is a matter for the trainers' initiative. They can obtain the required information by questionnaires, visits to ex-trainees at their places of work for discussions with them and their managers, holding meetings at the training centre for as many ex-trainees and managers as are able to attend.

EXAMPLE OF QUESTIONNAIRE ON THE EFFECTIVENESS OF CENTRAL TRAINING

1. Has training met the real needs of work? If not, why not?
2. What changes, if any, are needed in the aim, objectives, design, contents and methods?
3. Was any part of the programme superfluous?
4. Were any subjects covered insufficiently?
5. Was anything important omitted?
6. How effective were the training staff?
7. Are any other comments needed to be made on items such as the environment, accommodation, equipment, aids, administration, etc.

Notes
1. Support comments with examples.
2. Try to make any criticisms as constructive as possible, e.g. make positive suggestions for improvements.

EXERCISES ON DEVELOPING ABILITIES AND IMPROVING PERFORMANCE

EXERCISE 1

- In this chapter, refer to 'Developing People by Work Experience' (pages 139–142) and in particular the plan for a project assignment.
- Produce a project assignment based on a real situation in your own work that could be used for developmental purposes for an employee or employees, whom you manage.

EXERCISE 2

- In this chapter, refer to 'Developing People by Training' (pages 142–144) and in particular the section on objectives (Manager's Training Role, Stage 2).
- Using the example of objectives for training typists, write a list of objectives in the recommended form for a training course for your own employees.

EXERCISE 3

- In this chapter, refer to 'Managing the Training System' (pages 144–150). Imagine that you are a consultant required to assess how effectively a work-organization is managing its training function. List the criteria which you would use to make your judgement. It would be useful to express the criteria in question form. For example, do all staff involved in any way in the design and provision of training receive adequate training themselves for their training tasks?

SUGGESTED ANSWER FOR EXERCISE 3

1. Are requirements for effective performance clearly and comprehensively defined?
2. Is the performance of work regularly appraised as a basis for determining needs and action?
3. Is the design and provision of training based on a sound needs-assessment, i.e. who needs training? What kind of training?
4. Is training designed and provided cost-effectively in terms of:
   (a) clear definition of aims and objectives;
   (b) choosing and using the most appropriate forms and methods?
5. Do managers play a leading role in training design and provision, liaising with training staff?
6. Is there a sound system for assessing the effectiveness of training, i.e.
   (a) achievement of training aim and objectives;
   (b) ultimate effect on subsequent work-performance?
7. Is adequate training provided for all those in any way involved in the design and provision of training?
8. Are the costs of training planned, carefully monitored and known?
9. How satisfied are managers and ex-trainee employees with training provided?

CHAPTER 10

Caring for People at Work

BASIC QUESTIONS

1 Why is it extremely important that managers at all levels should pay particular attention to the health and safety of people at work?
2 What responsibilities do senior managers have for health and safety at work and what do they need to do in practice?
3 What responsibilities do junior managers have and what do they need to do in practice?
4 What are the reasons for lack of proper attention to health and safety and what can and should managers do about it?
5 What responsibilities do managers have for the welfare of their employees?
6 What positive steps can and should they take?
7 What particular skills does effective counselling require?

---

(1) HEALTH AND SAFETY

In recent decades amidst the ever-increasing volume of legislation designed to protect people at work the subject of health and safety has received particular attention. The Robens Report of 1972 and the establishment of the Health and Safety Executive (HSE) has initiated laws and codes of practice which pervade every aspect of health and safety in working life – potentially dangerous machinery and substances, noxious emissions, fire risks, overcrowding, ventilation, temperature, lighting, noise, stressful and health damaging equipment and practices, seating, etc. With the development of an increasingly complex, technological industrial society the science of ergonomics has grown in importance *vis-à-vis* health and safety at work. Ergonomics is concerned with problems of mutual adjustment between people and their work. Its purpose is to optimize the design of equipment, the environment and working practices for the well-being of employees and the effectiveness of working units.

Nevertheless, despite the efforts of ergonomists, the increase in legislation to protect people at work, the continual exhortation and intervention by the HSE and other bodies with an interest in the subject, current statistics give no cause for comfort or complacency. According to the latest reports produced by the HSE, on average every day two people are killed and some six thousand are injured at work. Each year about three-quarters of a million employees are away from work because of work-related illnesses. All of this adds up to a frightening total of over thirty million working days lost for reasons of health and safety.

These figures could be described as catastrophic, indicating a need for constant vigilance and much more effort, if any significant improvement is to be achieved. Apart from the very serious effects on individual employees and their families, employers suffer from loss of productivity and lowered morale and commitment. They may also have to face the consequences of infringing the law and attracting adverse publicity to themselves, because they are seen as employers who show little or no concern for the welfare of their employees.

The specific reasons for accidents and health problems at work are obviously varied. They may be caused by neglect on the part of employers or carelessness on the part of employees, or a combination of both. However, undoubtedly the major factor affecting the overwhelming majority of these incidents is attitude. People regularly do not approach the subject of health and safety with adequate care and attention. Insufficient imagination and foresight are applied to the subject. Time and again, investigations, show that management and employees were too complacent and failed to anticipate incidents that could have been avoided. Major disasters on the railway, at sea, and in industrial premises regularly point to main causes being a serious lack of attention to health and safety.

As with every industrial enterprise a strong lead must come from the top of the organization. After that there must be co-operation at all levels between managers and their work-groups.

The responsibilities of senior management are these:

1. To formulate and publish policy for health and safety at work, based on employment law and the guidelines laid down by the HSE.
2. To specify managerial responsibilities for health and safety.
3. To define practice for identifying hazards, assessing potential risks and the means for control.
4. To ensure that all employers in the organization are fully aware of the policy and provisions for health and safety and their individual responsibilities for putting them into effective practice.
5. To carry out regular checks and drills to ensure that all employees are continuously vigilant in their attention to health and safety matters.
6. To establish contingency plans and drills for possible major emergencies.
7. To involve staff at all levels in shaping policy and practice, especially lower grades who are mainly concerned with work and its dangers.
8. To consult with specialists, e.g. HSE inspectors, local environmental health officers, fire officers, for advice about health and safety measures, equipment, appliances, etc.
9. To review policy and practice regularly and to revise as may be necessary.
10. To maintain accurate records, covering all aspects of health and safety, and to make reports to the HSE as required by current employment law.
11. To measure the organization's performance in matters of health and safety in order to learn lessons from past mistakes and to be aware whether the provisions of organizational policy, HSE codes and governmental legislation are being met.
12. To provide adequate training for all staff with special responsibilities for health and safety at work.

Because junior managers are at the sharp end of operations and are in daily, regular contact with work-groups, they have an especially important role to play:

1. In the first place their own attitudes towards the subject must be positive. They must truly appreciate and believe in the importance of caring for the health and safety of the members of their teams and be constantly alert. They must set a good example. If they are seen not to care, how can they expect the people for whom they are responsible to take the subject seriously?

2. Communicating the requirements for health and safety at work, emphasizing its importance and taking necessary action starts with the induction of new employees and is continued thereafter by means of regular performance-appraisal discussions with individuals and regular discussions with work-groups as a whole.
3. Special attention should be given to newly appointed staff, especially if their work involves any potential hazards or risks, to ensure that they develop good habits for health and safety.
4. Health and safety should be a regular subject for the agenda of group meetings. Here managers can seek the views, advice and suggestions from their teams.
5. In addition to information acquired from discussions with individuals and groups managers need to be out and about observing for themselves. Regular checks should be made specifically to ensure that organizational policy and legal requirements are being met and above all to anticipate possible incidents before they occur.
6. To keep the importance of health and safety at work to the forefront of employers' attention a certain amount of propaganda can be useful, provided in the form of posters, films and talks by managers.
7. Managers at junior levels also need to keep records, covering all matters minor and major concerned with health and safety at work for purposes of any subsequent inquiries or legal proceedings and for general reference in the future.
8. Finally, training in health and safety is extremely important, so that managers may be fully aware of the requirements of employment law and for effective practice. Training should normally be arranged by senior management as part of the organizational policy for health and safety at work. If this is not done, then junior managers will have to take the initiative themselves and make representations to higher authority for health and safety training to be included in in-house training courses, or else to be provided by external training centres. At the same time, managers would be very well advised to take courses in the basics of first aid or at least to see that a member of their work-group is given this kind of training. Such knowledge and skill could make all the difference between life and death, as, for example, when resuscitation is needed.

(2) WELFARE

In discussing this subject, some texts debate the arguments for and against welfare. The case against apparently rests on two propositions, i.e. welfare needs can be adequately met from a wide variety of sources provided by central and local government and a whole range of other agencies; employees' personal problems are not the concern of the employer. This is a difficult position to maintain. No employers worth their salt could seriously maintain that the wellbeing of their employees is none of their business. Furthermore, the divide between life inside and outside of work is by no means clear-cut. Domestic problems regularly affect performance and behaviour at work and are inevitably, therefore, of concern to employers. Conversely, problems at work can affect life outside working hours.

Welfare covers very much more than providing good social, recreational and restaurant facilities, important though these may be. It requires a recognition by employers of the importance of the wellbeing of their employees and a readiness to give them help, support and advice as and when they may need this assistance. The welfare of employees in general organizational terms is mainly a responsibility for the personnel staff, and, in large organizations, for welfare specialists. As always, the first managerial contacts for employees are the leaders of their own work-groups. Junior managers, therefore, have a particularly important responsibility in attending to the welfare needs of the individuals in their teams.

The main question to consider is whether managers should take the initiative when they are aware that members of their team may need help with personal problems inside or outside work, or whether they should leave it to individuals to approach them for help and advice. Managers who care about the welfare of the members of their teams and are alert and observant may sense that something is wrong. They can ask: Are you all right? Is there anything I can do to help? without appearing intrusive. Whether people are inclined to consult their managers on welfare matters will depend very much on the manager's style and personality. If they trust and respect their managers as sensitive, warm-hearted, benevolent, approachable human beings, who will listen with empathy, they are quite likely to turn to their group-leaders for help with welfare matters. On the other hand, stern autocrats will seldom, if ever, be approached for this kind of assistance.

Helping people with welfare problems needs counselling skills, based on the skills of asking and listening regularly required in other interpersonal situations of work. In general, the manager's approach to discussions of welfare matters should be as follows:

1. Start by getting individuals to describe the problem.
2. Be aware that problems are not always as described *prima facie*. They are often affected by personal values, attitudes, assumptions, prejudices, emotions and perceptions. Skilful questioning and listening may reveal that the real problem lies elsewhere.
3. Do not adopt a parental role and offer immediate solutions, e.g. Why don't you . . . ? or, If I were you, I would . . . etc.
4. Using the open-question technique, help people to get a better understanding of their problems and any part they may play. Help them to find their own solutions by examining the range of possible options and choosing the most acceptable.
5. If the problem needs further assistance, refer the individuals to the appropriate source of help, e.g. the personnel department, welfare office, Citizen's Advice Bureau, CRUSE (for bereavement), RELATE (for marriage guidance).
6. Maintain strict confidence and assure those seeking counsel that their secrets are safe.

There are two particular welfare situations where managers do not need to wait until they are asked for help. People who are absent from work through prolonged illness are more than likely to feel low in spirits and cut off from their normal working environment. Most would welcome supportive gestures from their employers. Group-leaders or deputizing colleagues can do much to uplift the spirits of those who are ill and let them know that they are not forgotten by visiting them in hospital or home, if that is convenient and acceptable.

The loss of a close relative is an exceptionally distressing situation, causing grief, shock, depression and feelings of bewilderment. Managers and group-members can show their concern and support for bereaved colleagues by attending funerals as representatives of the employing organization. They may also be able to offer substantial assistance, if needed, during these very difficult times, in matters such as funeral arrangements and the various other actions that deaths entail.

EXERCISE ON HEALTH AND SAFETY AT WORK

This exercise is based on a talk on this subject. The details of the exercise are given at the end of Chapter 3, Interpersonal Skills, under the heading Exercise on Speaking to Groups (pages 163–166).

CHAPTER 11

Dealing with Unsatisfactory Performance

BASIC QUESTIONS

1 What essential steps must managers take before charging and punishing any employee for a breach of discipline?
2 Under what circumstances might an employee be suspended or dismissed for disciplinary reasons?
3 What essential steps must management take before it can be properly decided that an employee is incompetent?
4 Under what circumstances might an employee be dismissed for incompetence?

---

(1) DISCIPLINE

Despite managers' efforts to get the best from the members of their teams, there are likely to be occasions when somebody steps out of line. Managers are then obliged to intervene and take appropriate action. Dealing with disciplinary matters is one of the more unpleasant tasks of the manager's job. It is a negative diversion from their positive activities and may consume a considerable amount of time that could be much better spent for productive purposes. The Theory Y, democratic-participative style, advocated in this book as generally the most effective, is based on adult–adult relationships between managers and their staffs. If these managers do adopt a parental role, it is usually as the nurturing rather than the critical parent. Breaches of discipline compel such managers to adopt a role that goes against the grain of their preferred style. Nevertheless, in the interests of the achievement of the group's goals, the harmony of the group and the individuals themselves, they must not shirk this responsibility, distasteful though it might be. When a really serious offence has been committed, managers are left with no choice but to do something at once. Many breaches of discipline, however, are relatively minor or even trivial. There is a temptation, therefore, to wait a while and hope that things will improve. More often than not this is only putting off the evil day. If managers fail to take prompt action to nip any instance of delinquency in the bud, they could well find themselves facing much more trouble at some future time.

Managers may not be able to anticipate any sudden, unexpected incidents, but they can and should be alert to spot any signs of incipient or persistent bad conduct and to do something about it, before it develops into a more serious offence. It requires the GOYA technique. Managers who come out of their offices and move around regularly amongst their work-groups give themselves opportunities to observe whether anything is happening that could become a disciplinary issue. Is employee A being over-familiar with and a nuisance to the female staff? Is employee B failing to observe rules laid down for health and safety? Employee C's breath seems to smell of alcohol on several occasions. A quiet talk in the privacy of the manager's office may well ensure that behaviour does not develop into conduct that requires formal disciplinary and punitive action. The transgressions of employees A and B should cease there and then, if they have any sense. Employee C, however, may well have a drink problem that needs to be referred for specialist advice and help.

Whilst prevention is always better than cure where disciplinary matters are concerned, there will obviously be cases from time to time when managers must resort to formal procedures. These procedures should be based on the criteria-evidence-judgement system, i.e.

1. The standards of conduct expected of employees should be published. A copy of these requirements should be given to all newly appointed employees during the induction phase as a condition of employment. Published directives about conduct would normally include matters that are commonly recognized as adversely affecting the productive performance of work and the harmony and wellbeing of work-groups, e.g. punctuality, attendance, careless, negligent or dangerous actions, excessive intake of alcohol, drugs, smoking in restricted areas, sexual harassment, racism, etc. Obviously rules of conduct cannot cover every possible contingency, such as, for example, brawling, use of foul language, stealing, indecency. Such misdemeanours do not need to be

embraced specifically in the published rules. They can be covered by a general provision such as ' . . . any other behaviour that management considers to be a breach of required conduct'.

2. Before any disciplinary action is taken, cases must be investigated thoroughly and with complete fairness. As in the law courts, accused persons should be considered as innocent until the weight of evidence leaves no reasonable doubts about guilt. Witnesses may be produced for the prosecution and defence. Employees accused of offences must be given every chance to state their case and to be accompanied by a union official or colleague, if they so wish.

3. In passing judgement and deciding action, managers must take account of any mitigating circumstances and employees' past behaviour. The employee who has been persistently late in recent times may have domestic problems that are the real cause of the unpunctuality. This does not alter the facts of the employee's time-keeping, but it does indicate that this is probably much more than a straightforward disciplinary issue.

4. Except for the most serious breaches of discipline, employees should not be dismissed for a first offence. Warnings should be given to confirm management's judgement that an offence has been committed, that an improvement is required and that the consequences for the offending employee could be serious, if the bad conduct is repeated, e.g. suspension or dismissal. Normally, a first warning would be oral. Subsequent warnings should be in writing.

5. Managers should keep accurate records of all disciplinary hearings and action taken. They may well be needed as evidence, should offences be repeated, or if cases are referred to industrial tribunals. Records should be written immediately, whilst the investigation is still fresh in the memory.

Managers' demeanour and investigatory skills are as important as the procedures described above. However irritated or angry they may feel, they must do everything possible to curb their emotions. No matter how they may feel inside they must present a calm, cool, controlled demeanour during hearings. In particular, they need to apply the skills of asking and listening, already discussed in Chapter 3. Questions should be simple and open (how, when, what, where, who, why), probing in following up clues given in the answers, not suggestive of possible answers. Meanings should be checked and clarified. Finally, investigating managers should summarize what has been said and should ask the employees concerned whether the summary is fair and accurate.

Disciplinary cases can lead to all kinds of problems for management. They need to be conducted with exceptional skill and fairness and in accordance with the current provisions of employment law. Failure to do so could result in hearings before industrial tribunals and verdicts against defaulting employers. It goes without saying that managers' own conduct should be exemplary. They are on very thin ice when disciplining their staffs if their own conduct leaves something to be desired.

(2) INCOMPETENCE

Competent performance, as we have already seen when discussing job analysis, implies that employees are ready, willing and able to meet the specified requirements of their jobs in terms of knowledge, skills, attitudes and personal attributes. If managers judge that employees' performance is incompetent this should mean that:

1. The requirements for effective performance have been carefully, comprehensively and accurately defined.
2. They have been communicated to employees, who understand and accept these requirements.
3. Performance has been regularly appraised.
4. The evidence of performance appraisal has revealed conclusive evidence of a failure to meet the specified requirements of jobs.
5. Managers have advised employees of their incompetence and possible consequences. They have done everything possible to help incompetent employees to achieve the necessary improvement, e.g. counselling, training on and off the job, etc.
6. Despite this assistance, performance has not improved; it has remained at an unacceptable level over a period of time. Managers have concluded that further improvement to achieve required levels of performance is no longer possible.

    Some employees could be incompetent in all aspects, e.g. lacking the necessary knowledge and skills and approaching work with the wrong attitudes. Some may be doing the best they can, but their best still is not good enough. They are simply not up to the job. Some may be capable, but show no interest or enthusiasm, are incurably lazy, regularly careless or negligent, or continually upset work-colleagues or clients.

If managers consider that incompetent performance has been conclusively proven, they may legally dismiss employees. It is always possible, of course, that some employees will not take this judgement lying down. They may challenge conclusions and decisions and seek redress in the courts. This is one important reason why managers should follow the systematic procedures described above. If they do not do so, they may encounter all kinds of difficulties, if their decisions are subsequently challenged and they are required to justify their conclusions and actions.

Finally, in connection with incompetent performance it is appropriate to emphasize a point that was made about employee-selection in Chapter 6. The prediction of future competence of performance is an abiding problem. Mistakes can easily be made. It is very easy to be wise after the event. People who appeared to be quite suitable during the selection process may confound the selectors' judgements by proving to be incompetent after taking up their appointments. All the same, every incompetent employee who slips through the selection net could be seen as an example of faulty selection. This is why employers need to make the selection process as cost-effective as it can possibly be, investing adequate resources and training selectors. Whilst the main task is to appoint suitable employees, selectors must also be concerned not to appoint people whose incompetence could cause all kinds of problems in the future. Mistakes in employee-selection can, of course, be mitigated or rectified by a system of probationary appointments.

EXERCISE ON DISCIPLINE

- Carefully read the case-studies. They were originally used for training bank managerial staff in the management of people, but the situations described could occur in any work situation.
- For the purposes of this exercise, assume that the facts are much as stated in the scripts and that no other significant evidence emerges.
- If you were the manager of these employees how would you approach each case and what action would you take?

DISCIPLINE INTERVIEW NO. 1 *Script for Manager*

Employee B

As manager of the branch you are about to interview B, one of your clerical staff. B has been the subject of a strong complaint by Mrs Q, a very wealthy, elderly local widow, who keeps large current and deposit accounts with the bank. You cannot afford to have her upset, although frankly she is by no means one of your favourite customers. At worst she could withdraw her account and spread adverse comments amongst her circle of wealthy local bridge-playing friends. She came to see you in a very angry mood with the following charge.

Last week she was in your branch with two of her prize Pekinese, when they were attacked by a nasty mongrel. This led to a very unpleasant dog fight. Her friend Mrs Y was at the counter cashing a cheque and over-heard the clerk Mr B make a very offensive remark to a colleague: 'It's about time that silly old bitch kept her dogs at home and preferably stayed there herself.' Her friend wouldn't make up a story like that. Something like that must have been said. Nor is that the end of the story. When Mrs Q went up to B to demand an instant apology, she met even further rudeness. B denied the story, said that he was busy with another customer and she would have to wait, that she shouldn't believe second-hand gossip and that Mrs Y needs to 'wash her ears out'. All this happened at a very busy time in front of a crowd of customers. Mrs Q was most embarrassed and very angry. She supposed that this was typical of today's breed of ill-mannered youth, but expected better standards from the bank.

B joined the bank only twelve months ago on first appointment from school. He/she is rather brash and over-confident perhaps, but so far his/her work has been very promising and there have been no complaints about conduct. You cannot avoid taking some action, but you have some sympathy with B and do not want to crush his/her spirits.

DISCIPLINE CASE NO. 1   *Script for B*

Employee B

This is your first job and you have been at the bank for twelve months. So far you seem to have settled in well and made good progress. Unfortunately, you now have to see the manager for what looks like being an 'on the carpet' disciplinary hearing. This is your story: last week a certain Mrs Q was in the bank with two of her nasty little Pekinese (sometimes she even brings three). They became involved in a scrap with another dog, as they usually do, given half a chance. They reflect their owner's character. It all happened at a very busy time and caused quite a scene. You personally do not like dogs and you are, in fact, afraid of them when they fight – all traceable to a very unpleasant incident in a shop with an Alsatian when you were three years old. All the staff complain about Mrs Q and her dogs and you probably did mutter something under your breath. Anyway, whatever you said, it seems it was overheard by Mrs Y, whom you were serving at the time. She's a close friend of Mrs Q, and obviously she went and told her that you had made a comment. The next thing you knew was a verbal onslaught from Mrs Q when you were serving the next customer. You cannot remember what was said, but Mrs Q was certainly very offensive to you and said something about the standards of the modern generation. You tried to calm her down and asked her not to believe what her friend had said and to wait until you had finished serving your customer. You might have argued back perhaps, but Mrs Q has been asking for it for a long time and it's time somebody told her a few home truths.

SUGGESTED ANSWER

Case No. 1   Employee B

This is a fairly serious case because an important customer has been antagonized unnecessarily. As usual in such cases, arguments over what exactly was said are largely futile and easily develop into an 'oh yes you did – oh no I didn't' conflict. B does not deny muttering something uncomplimentary which apparently was overheard.

Suggested response by the manager:

1. Employees regularly have views about awkward customers. Undoubtedly, Mrs Q is one of these. All the same, employees must keep their views to themselves and certainly not give any indications either by words or looks to customers about their feelings.
2. B's behaviour was very irresponsible and thoughtless. It has put the manager in a very difficult position of having to placate Mrs Q.
3. So far B's performance has been very promising in his first job. However, he must learn to curb any tendencies to behave like this. Effective performance requires more than professional competence alone. It must be supported by the right attitudes and behaviour.
4. As this is a first offence B will be given a strong oral warning about conduct to be recorded in the personal file.

DISCIPLINE CASE No. 2   *Script for Manager*

Employee C

As branch manager, you are about to carry out a disciplinary interview with a 30-year-old member of the clerical staff. The case was reported to you as follows by the accountant:

   Last week the accountant caught C embracing and fondling one of the women clerks in an upstairs room now used for storing files and other documents. He had noticed that they were often missing at the same time and had gone to look for them. His suspicions had been aroused for some time because of amatory behaviour between the two when they should have been getting on with their work, e.g. glances, nods, winks and generally flirtatious conduct. Unfortunately, the case is further complicated because both C and the woman clerk in question are married, but not to each other. It has the makings of a scandal and needs to be dealt with firmly. The accountant describes C as something of an office Romeo. He has an eye for the girls and this is not the first time he's been involved in affairs. Apart from 'chatting up' female members of staff, he was apparently mixed up in a similar kind of situation with a married woman at his former branch. His personal file records an oral warning by the manager at the time.

DISCIPLINE CASE No. 2   *Script for C*

Employee C

You are about to see the manager on a serious disciplinary charge reported to him by the accountant.

It arose because the accountant burst into an upstairs store-room and caught you larking about with Mrs W, a clerical colleague. You are now being accused of having an affair with her and carrying on during office hours. Actually you had gone upstairs at her request to help her find a file which she needed to locate. You freely admit that you are both very friendly and that you regularly see her outside working hours. But that is no business of the bank. What the accountant and the manager do not know is that you left your wife about a month ago and you now live alone in a bachelor flat. Mrs W is also at odds with her husband, although her situation is complicated by children. Nevertheless, she is seriously considering leaving him and who knows, she could move in with you.

This relationship is not affecting your work or hers, but the situation is made much worse by the accountant, a crusty, old, passed-over bachelor who is sex-starved and very jealous. He's making a mountain out of a molehill and has grossly exaggerated his account of what we were supposed to have been doing.

SUGGESTED ANSWER

Case No. 2   Employee C

This is the more serious case of the two.

Suggested response by the manager:

1. C's behaviour is not only affecting his own performance, it is having a potentially disruptive influence on the rest of the work-group.
2. C's contention that an employee's private life is none of the employer's business is not disputed. However, it is the employer's concern if it affects work and in this case it does.
3. C has behaved similarly on previous occasions and was given an oral warning by a former manager.
4. C will be given a formal written warning, emphasizing the ultimate possible sanctions if the behaviour does not cease forthwith, i.e. suspension or dismissal.

The manager should also speak sternly to Mrs X about her part in the case. She should be given an oral warning.

Author's Summary

The question with which this book has been concerned is: what do managers have to do and to be in order to be effective leaders of work-groups? The answer that I have given can be summarized as follows:

1. Amongst the various personnel-tasks that managers have to carry out, the two most important are:
   (a) to identify and recruit people who can meet the requirements for the effective performance of work. Mistakes in employee-selection can lead to all kinds of serious problems and consequences. Therefore, employers must ensure that their selection methods are as sound as possible. Above all, managers must be trained in selection methods and especially in interviewing;
   (b) continuously to develop and to improve the performance of re-cruited employees. In times of rapid change in technology and work-methods, this is especially important. The development of human resources through work experience and training is not only necessary for the achievement of organizational goals, it also helps to meet employees' expectations and needs, and is, therefore, a motivating influence.
2. Sound judgement is the foundation for all the personnel tasks of management. It requires the following system:
   (a) definition of the criteria for effective performance of work;
   (b) acquisition of as much valid evidence as possible of potential and actual performance;
   (c) comparison of evidence and criteria as a basis for decisions and action.
3. The main elements of the judgement system are:
   (a) job-analysis – to define the requirements for effective performance in terms of the job and the job-holder;
   (b) performance-appraisal – to assess how far these requirements are being met as a basis for future action.
4. The effectiveness of the framework described above depends on the prevailing leadership style, behaviour and performance of managers in the human aspects of their job. They must:

(a) develop their knowledge of human behaviour, awareness of their own behaviour, and a high level of interpersonal skills as a basis for effective practice;
(b) have regular performance-appraisal discussions with the individual members of their teams so that their needs are kept under constant review and appropriate and timely action is taken;
(c) be constantly out and about amongst the members of their teams to observe, ask, listen and gather firsthand information as a basis for the many and various decisions that typify the manager's job.

Some managers will naturally be more gifted than others in the human aspects of the job. Nevertheless, all managers need to study these subjects by reading and through training courses so as to lay sound foundations for continuous development through the practice of actual work.

What I have described is the systematic management of people at work – the only means by which effectiveness may be achieved.

Index